Saline District Library
W9-ASB-359

George and Barbara Bush

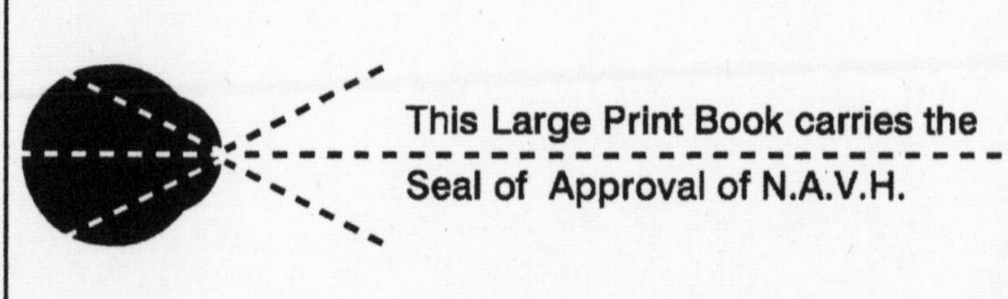
This Large Print Book carries the
Seal of Approval of N.A.V.H.

GEORGE AND BARBARA BUSH

A GREAT AMERICAN LOVE STORY

BY THEIR GRANDDAUGHTER,
ELLIE LEBLOND SOSA
AND KELLY ANNE CHASE

Foreword by President George W. Bush

THORNDIKE PRESS
A part of Gale, a Cengage Company

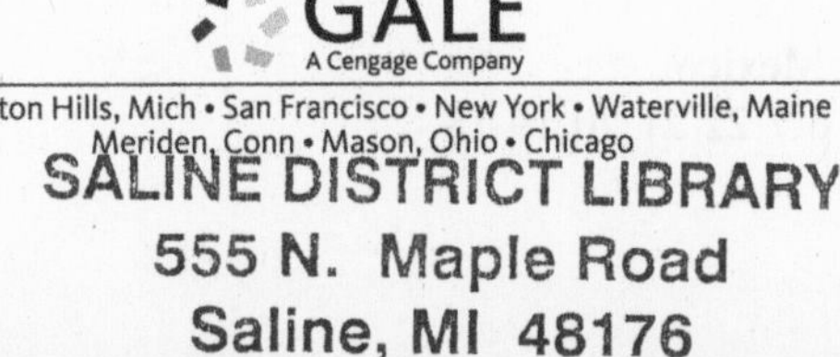

Farmington Hills, Mich • San Francisco • New York • Waterville, Maine
Meriden, Conn • Mason, Ohio • Chicago

Thorndike Press, a part of Gale, a Cengage Company.

Thorndike Press® Large Print Biographies and Memoirs.
The text of this Large Print edition is unabridged.
Other aspects of the book may vary from the original edition.
Set in 16 pt. Plantin.

**LIBRARY OF CONGRESS CIP DATA ON FILE.
CATALOGUING IN PUBLICATION FOR THIS BOOK
IS AVAILABLE FROM THE LIBRARY OF CONGRESS**

ISBN-13: 978-1-4328-5757-8 (hardcover)

Published in 2018 by arrangement with Down East Books

Printed in Mexico
1 2 3 4 5 6 7 22 21 20 19 18

To Ganny and Gampy,
may your love for each other
inspire us all.

When **she** shall die
take **her** and cut **her** out into stars
and **she** shall make the
face of heaven so fine
that all the world will be
in love with night
and pay no worship to the garish sun.

— ORIGINALLY BY WILLIAM SHAKESPEARE,
BUT EDITED SLIGHTLY BY
PRESIDENT GEORGE H. W. BUSH
FOR BARBARA BUSH'S FUNERAL ON
SATURDAY, APRIL 21, 2018.

CONTENTS

FOREWORD 13
ACKNOWLEDGMENTS 17
INTRODUCTION 19
AUTHORS' NOTE 25

1. They Meet 27
2. Poppy. 36
3. Courting 55
4. Phillips Academy 61
5. Bar. 67
6. "I'm Going In." 87
7. Secret's Safe. 102
8. Secret's Out 105
9. Halfway Across the World 114
10. Word from Home 125
11. A Time for Celebration 141
12. Then There Were Three 151
13. Promises of West Texas 167
14. Friends, Faith, and Family. 185

15. Off They Go! 203
16. Diving Head-First into the
World of Politics 223
17. Distance, It's Good for
the Heart 244
18. Back in the Races 259
19. First Couple 285
20. FLFW & FFLFW 305
21. Anchor to Windward 317

SOURCES 331
ABOUT THE AUTHORS 357

FOREWORD

PRESIDENT GEORGE W. BUSH

My niece, Ellie, chose to write about a subject dear to our entire family: the love story of George and Barbara Bush. The longest-married Presidential couple in history has been an inspiration and example to Laura and me, to my siblings, and — I like to think — to many of our fellow citizens. I'm thankful that Ellie has recorded their relationship in these pages.

When asked on his 90th birthday what the happiest moment in his life had been, Dad said that it was the day that he married my mother. In this book, Ellie writes about the moment 17-year-old George Bush was struck by the beauty of Barbara Pierce and wanted to ask her to dance, but he didn't know how to waltz. She shares the love letters that the young Navy pilot and Smith College coed wrote each other during World War II — and of their secret engagement during Dad's leave in 1943.

Ellie also illustrates how the young couple's obvious affection made the engagement a poorly kept secret. As my father wrote to my mother before their wedding, "I love you, precious, with all my heart and to know that you love me means my life. How often I have thought about the immeasurable joy that will be ours some day. How lucky our children will be to have a mother like you." How prescient Dad was.

I once asked my mother how she and my father managed to stay happily married for more than seventy years. "Both of us have always been willing to go three-quarters of the way," she explained. Because they were more committed to their marriage than they were to themselves, they were each willing to sacrifice their own needs in order to satisfy the other's. Throughout my life, Mother and Dad demonstrated truly selfless love. And Ellie brings that love to life in this book, across dozens of cities and nearly as many decades. From the shared pain of losing a child to the triumphs of the Presidency, when they needed each other most, Mother and Dad were both willing to go three-quarters of the way — and every step of the way, their marriage emerged stronger.

On April 17, 2018, Barbara Pierce Bush spent her final hours the way she wanted:

holding hands with the love of her life. Before Mom left this Earth, she said her soul was settled. She believed in God and Heaven above. And she knew that one day her soulmate, George H. W. Bush, would join her there for eternity.

ACKNOWLEDGMENTS

Writing this book has been a fascinating and fulfilling journey and there are a number of people who helped us along the way. We must thank the dedicated, passionate staff at the George Bush Presidential Library and Museum: Warren and Mary Finch, Chris Pembelton, and everyone who worked behind the scenes. We are grateful to our editor Michael Steere for his guidance as well as the hardworking team behind him at Down East Books and Rowman & Littlefield.

We are thankful and indebted to Uncle George, for offering his unique perspective on Gampy and Ganny's love story; Jon Meacham, who gifted us wisdom and knowledge in our research; Aunt Nan Ellis and Uncle Scott Pierce, who took time to share their stories; Sandra Bush for providing her editorial expertise; Jean Becker, who is our jack of all trades, gatekeeper, and biggest cheerleader; Mom and Uncle Neil, who read each chapter aloud to Gampy while he was in the hospital and lent their support and encouragement along the way.

Thank you to our husbands, Nick and Sam, for being our sounding boards, proofreaders, and loving (and patient) companions.

And of course, Gampy and Ganny, President George H. W. and Mrs. Barbara Bush, who have shown us how to always think about the other guy and live a life full of gratitude, kindness, friendship, loyalty, and love.

INTRODUCTION

The first memory I have of my grandparents together happened during a momentous occasion. It was 1992 and we were in Houston, Texas, at the Republican National Convention, and my grandfather had just been nominated for reelection. He was about to enter into the general election campaign with the hopes of serving as president of the United States for four more years. I was on stage along with my parents, aunts, uncles, and cousins, and Gampy and Ganny (as we call them) were standing in front of us.

I can see them now — my grandmother in her blue suit and pearls beside my grandfather in his suit and red tie. I was just about the right height, waist high, to see them instinctively reach for each other's hands — two linked silhouettes against a backdrop of confetti and cheers.

A few years prior, my mom, Doro Bush

Koch, moved from Portland, Maine, to Washington, D.C., with me and my brother, Sam. My parents had recently separated and my mom longed to be near hers. As a young mother raising two sometimes mischievous children, she relied on her parents' love and support and as a result we were frequent visitors to the White House.

Photographs from that time reveal Sam and me all over the White House — running through the long corridors, leaving a trail of toys and crumbs. We spent many weekends there, and the White House became like a second home for us, as odd as that sounds. It was during those first few years in Washington that I grew especially close to my grandparents.

Today, I live in Boston, Massachusetts, with my husband. When we moved here in 2014 we weren't sure how long we'd stay, but the greatest perk of living in Boston has been the short hour-and-a-half drive to my grandparents' summer home in Kennebunkport, Maine.

We spend almost every weekend there during the summer months. Kennebunkport, and specifically Walker's Point, is heaven for me. It means summer breezes, delicious seafood, and most importantly, the place where our family comes together during the warm summer months. Naturally, it is where my husband and I decided to be married in the fall of 2014. It is also in Kennebunkport where I have had the privilege of being a witness to my grandparents' relationship.

As they started growing older, my grandfather didn't mind staying home at night with my grandmother and watching a movie, but Ganny believed it was important for both of them to stay active. She accepted invitations for cocktail parties and scheduled dinners with family and friends. When the long dinner table at Walker's Point was crowded and noisy, Ganny would interrupt: "Please repeat that for Gampy!" She'd quiet everyone down to ask Gampy his thoughts on whatever it was we were talking about.

During those years, she never let him retreat.

In researching this book, that guiding principle — being strong when the other is weak, speaking up when the other is quiet, being patient when the other is hurting — surfaces throughout their marriage. They loyally carried each other through World War II, a move to a new part of the country, the tragic death of a child, the ups and downs of politics, personal battles with depression, and public scrutiny and loss.

In reading notes jotted on paper and glancing through scrapbooks of precious materials gathered over ninety years, I found that it was also the small gestures that have carried a lot of weight: a quick letter to say I love you, a phone call when you know the other is lonely, or the touch of a familiar hand during a stressful time.

Toward the end of the research for this book, my grandparents had been in and out of the hospital. When my grandmother was sick, my grandfather sat by her bedside, his arm outstretched holding her hand. I remembered that image captured by that five-year-old little girl.

My grandmother passed away just a week after conducting a final interview for this book, and she was still bright and candid — and in love with my grandfather. "You have to go 75 percent of the way," she offered when asked for marital advice. "Be thoughtful and make things nice for your husband or wife . . . it's a two-way street."

She continued, "I believe I've had a very happy marriage and I'm having a happy marriage."

Would she change anything? I asked. "I would have been nicer, thinner, smarter, more beautiful, more educated, I mean, all those things," she said, her voice slightly rough as she made everyone in the room laugh. "No, I wouldn't have changed anything. You're not going to talk to anyone any happier."

"I have no secrets," she said finally. She felt proud of the story she and my grandfather had written, as she should, but I believe there is one more to tell.

While there have been countless books produced about my beloved grandparents, the story of their decades-long love affair has never been written. This is not a comprehensive account of their life together, but rather a tribute to what can only be considered a great American love story.

— Ellie LeBlond Sosa

AUTHORS' NOTE

For this book, the authors interviewed Barbara Bush at Walker's Point in Kennebunkport, Maine, and at her home in Houston, Texas. They also referenced her memoirs as well as President George H. W. Bush's autobiography, *Looking Forward.* Throughout the book, the reader will find a number of letters, diary entries, and newspaper clippings, and many of these items were collected from the George Bush Presidential Library and Museum in College Station, Texas, as well as a few from the Bush family's personal collection. Almost all of the photographs in the book were provided by the George Bush Presidential Library and Museum.

One:
They Meet

August 2017

On a late summer morning, they are at home in Kennebunkport, Maine. Swift swirls of cold slide through the air reminding locals of the season's imminent switch. Out front, her garden is still in bloom, colors of petals slowly darkening on the tips of green stems. The faded shingled home that has been in his family for a century is so close to the ocean it seems fastened only to the rocks beneath it.

While he rests, she sits on the porch that faces east, a row of windows reveals where the sun rises each morning over the rough Atlantic surf. How many times they must have looked out at the marvel beyond this old home. Today, though, she sits with her back to the water she's known since that first visit seventy-four years ago when she was eighteen years old.

With increased age, it seems fewer things accumulate that hold true importance.

She pulls her legs up on the ottoman and rolls her oxygen to her side. Typically the dogs would be next to her, loyally tucked beneath her hand and pressed close. For now, they're stowed in the bedroom, where they can't bother inquisitive guests that have just arrived. Over nine decades old, a fascinating life, with so many stories to tell — where to begin? Luckily, she hasn't lost an ounce of the candor she is so well-known for. "Let's just get on with it," she said. With that, First Lady Barbara Bush recounted when she was introduced to the love of her life seventy-six years ago and everything changed — the night she met George H. W. Bush.

Over time, those things with short importance will loosen their hold of you, and only the most powerful moments remain.

December 1941

"We always had to go into Mother's room and talk when we got home. Otherwise, she could not sleep and, I believe she was smart enough to know that in the night, you are willing to tell all. If she waited until the next day, she knew she'd get one-syllable answers."

— BARBARA BUSH

In Rye, New York, Barbara Pierce entered her parents' bedroom, a required ritual after an evening out. It was late — and it had been dark for hours thanks to the December sun's increasingly limited appearance — but the enchanted sixteen-year-old buzzed like she'd only just awoke. She had met the most "heavenly boy," she gushed. Earlier that night, Barbara was invited to the Greenwich Country Club's Christmas dance. The white Georgian Colonial sparkled with holiday decor, and the band rolled out an upbeat set list of big band hits. Dances were social hubs for young people in the 1940s, and according to Barbara, "In those days you went with one person, but you danced with lots of people."

The wintry dance in Greenwich was full of music, holiday lights, and hopeful youth; however, an added urgency hung in the air. The attack on Pearl Harbor had occurred weeks before. Although there was talk of the United States joining, many felt removed from the fighting in Europe. The average household's brush with the war was during Edward R. Murrow's evening broadcasts that began in 1940. His rooftop transmissions, beginning with "This . . . is London" and ending with "Good night, and good luck" seemed like stories from a distant land, even for the generation who would come to be named after the war.

On this particular night in Connecticut, the looming uncertainty of war was for an evening distant, and at the end of a winding drive, the Greenwich Country Club was a welcome diversion from the decisions ahead. Some of the men in the room had made up their minds; they were determined to go off to war. Perhaps the overall unpredictability of one's future aided in the carefree nature of the dance. Chatter was noisy and light, and cutting in on a dancing couple was encouraged because you might as well take a chance.

Barbara Pierce embraced the free-spirited dance. She wore an off-the-shoulder red and green evening dress and moved across the room laughing, chatting, and dancing. Her short, wavy chestnut hair, round hazel eyes, and spontaneity caught the attention of one seventeen-year-old who thought she was "the life of the party."

Who's that? asked a young George

"Poppy" Bush.

That's Barbara Pierce from Rye, said Jack Wozencraft, a mutual friend who then offered an introduction.

Poppy gladly accepted. Although she was dancing with someone else, Barbara was intrigued by Jack's invitation.

Across the room she followed him to discover that Poppy Bush was tall, handsome, and friendly. Less important to Barbara, he also had a limited dance repertoire, so when the band transitioned into a waltz they moved off the floor to chat. George told Barbara Pierce from Rye that he grew up in Greenwich, and now he was a senior at Phillips Academy. Barbara relayed that she was in school at Ashley Hall in Charleston, home for winter break.

To this day, Barbara can't remember much of what she thought to be a fifteen-minute conversation at the Greenwich Country Club, but the memory of drifting home that night, glowing with excitement the way young people do, so effortlessly and fearlessly falling for a person they barely know, was still fresh in her mind seven decades later.

Back in her parents' bedroom, Pauline Pierce watched her daughter closely as she so willingly told her story. The routine was

George and Barbara at a dance.

the same for all four of Pauline's children. She'd smell their breath and hair — searching for traces of cigarette smoke, which wasn't allowed. Then she'd inquire about their evening out, extracting any details she could from the dimmed room.

"Can't this wait until morning?" Barbara's father, Marvin Pierce, called from the next bed. They were keeping him up, but Pauline knew the nightly inspections were crucial. She was the family disciplinarian after all and served as a watchdog over her household, making sure her daughters checked the appropriate boxes on their journey into womanhood. She knew if she waited until morning, she'd have missed out on critical information.

Pauline did wait until morning to make a few phone calls. She found out that Poppy came from a "very nice family," which she recited to Barbara the next day. Her mother's quick investigative work and resulting approval surprisingly did not deter Barbara, as it normally would have. The only thought on Barbara's mind was when she would encounter Poppy Bush from Greenwich again.

LOVE AT FIRST SIGHT?

"Was it love at first sight?" I asked Ganny over the summer after she had finished telling the tale of my grandparents' first encounter.

"It was for me," she said quickly. "I was mad about him."

When I inquired if the feeling was mutual, her answer was classic Ganny: "You gotta ask him."

Love at first sight or not, I am so thankful for that moment. From their love grew a big family, who all look up to my grandparents' faithful partnership. Together, Ganny and Gampy developed a set of principles that we all strive to uphold — not because we've been told to do so, but because we've had the privilege of witnessing two full, extraordinary lives and are inspired by the example they've set.

Think about the other guy is repeated over and over in the Bush family. At a young age, I remember understanding, mostly by example, to not worry so much about what you don't have, but think about what you do have and how you can use that to help others. Service has meant all kinds of things in our family: from volunteering at homeless shelters on holidays, or, on somewhat of a larger scale, starting our own organizations serving others. No matter how small or big, we have all had our hands in service.

When the entire extended family gets together, which seems to be less often these days, I look around and admire the passionate group of individuals who came from my grandparents. I can't help but think of that night in Greenwich seven decades ago, and how I am forever grateful Gampy spotted Ganny across the room and needed to find out who she was. He felt something when he saw her. I think, it must have been love.

Two:
Poppy

August 2017

President George H. W. Bush rests on his stone patio in Kennebunkport, Maine. He closes his eyes and tilts his head toward the sun. He's listening to his aide read to him — most likely a piece of historical nonfiction pulled off the shelf. Inside his summer home, and many miles away at his house in Houston, bookcases are stocked with stories about former presidents, first ladies, wars, and politics — each prominently displayed spine binds legacies of leaders past.

When asked about his legacy,
President Bush told author
David Baldacci close to a decade
ago: "I've banned the 'L' word. I just
think it's better to let history sort out
what you got right and what you
got wrong. But that doesn't mean
you don't care."

Now in Maine, he sits and listens. The nearby ocean slams on the ancient, jagged coastline before retreating back. The Northeast's waterways are notoriously dangerous but the powerful sea has always been a source of comfort for President Bush. When he was young, arriving in Maine meant adventures with his older brother, Prescott ("Pres"), and off the coast of Kennebunkport, he learned how to fish and steer a boat. Shutting his eyes, he can almost puzzle together the tiny pieces of memories that flutter like movie reels. Amid the crash of surf are the voices of young boys playing. For a moment, he can go back to 1933.

Summer 1933

The icy Atlantic waters surrounding the family compound in Kennebunkport have always dictated the day's adventures. When the tide retreated, George and his older brother Pres explored nearby tidal pools full of sea-dwelling creatures that hide beneath the tawny seaweed. On days when the weather turned (as it did frequently), they'd run inside and watch the storms pass from the shingled house on the coast — waves lunging at rocks and rain pounding at the windows, as they huddled inside playing board games and tiddlywinks. At night,

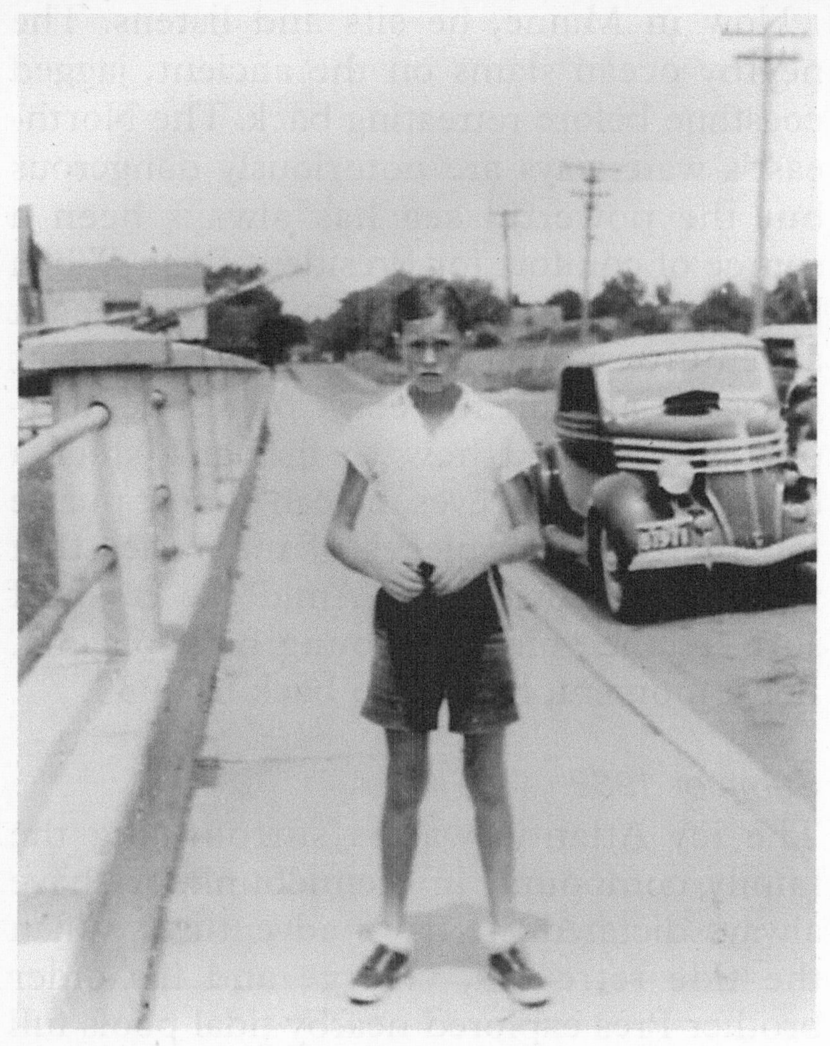

Young George in Kennebunkport.

thousands of white stars studded the black sky as George fell asleep listening to the tidal breath of the sleeping watery giant.

Maine was George H. W. Bush's childhood summer paradise.

The peninsula was purchased by George's

maternal great-grandfather, David Davis Walker and his son George Herbert Walker in 1902. They erected two matching mansions, and every summer George's family

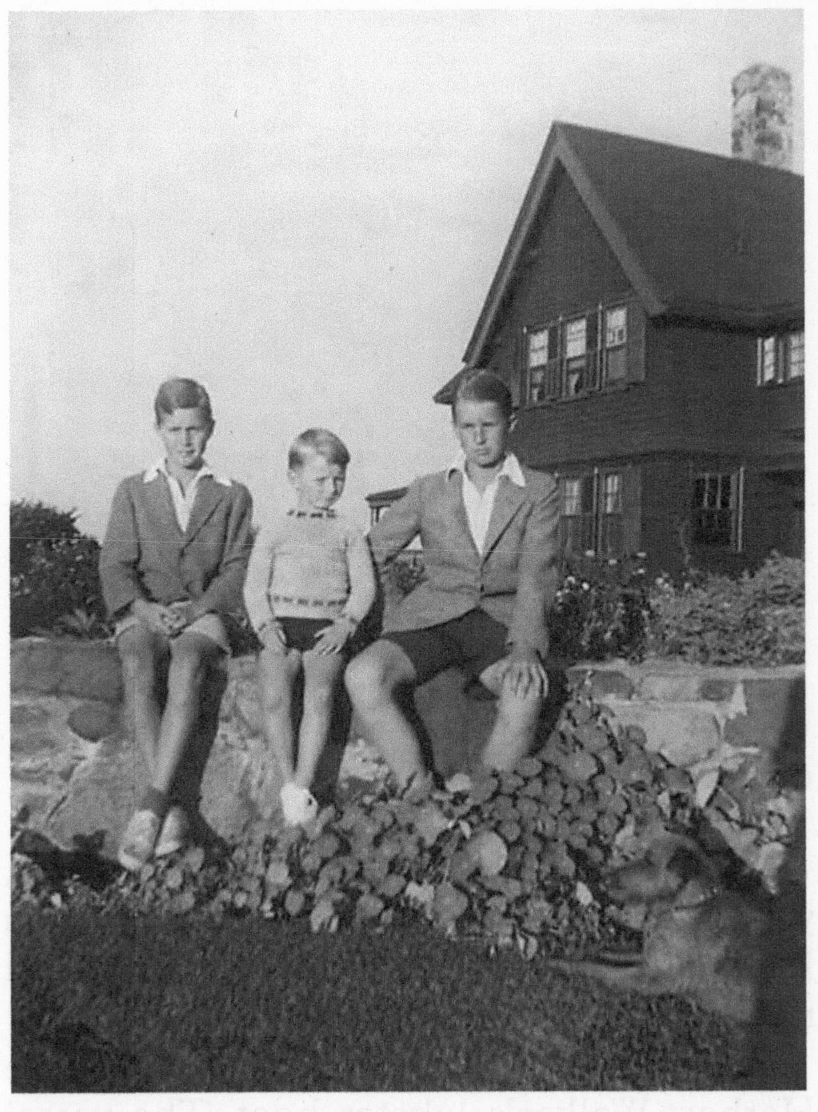

George, Johnny, and Pres as young boys in Maine.

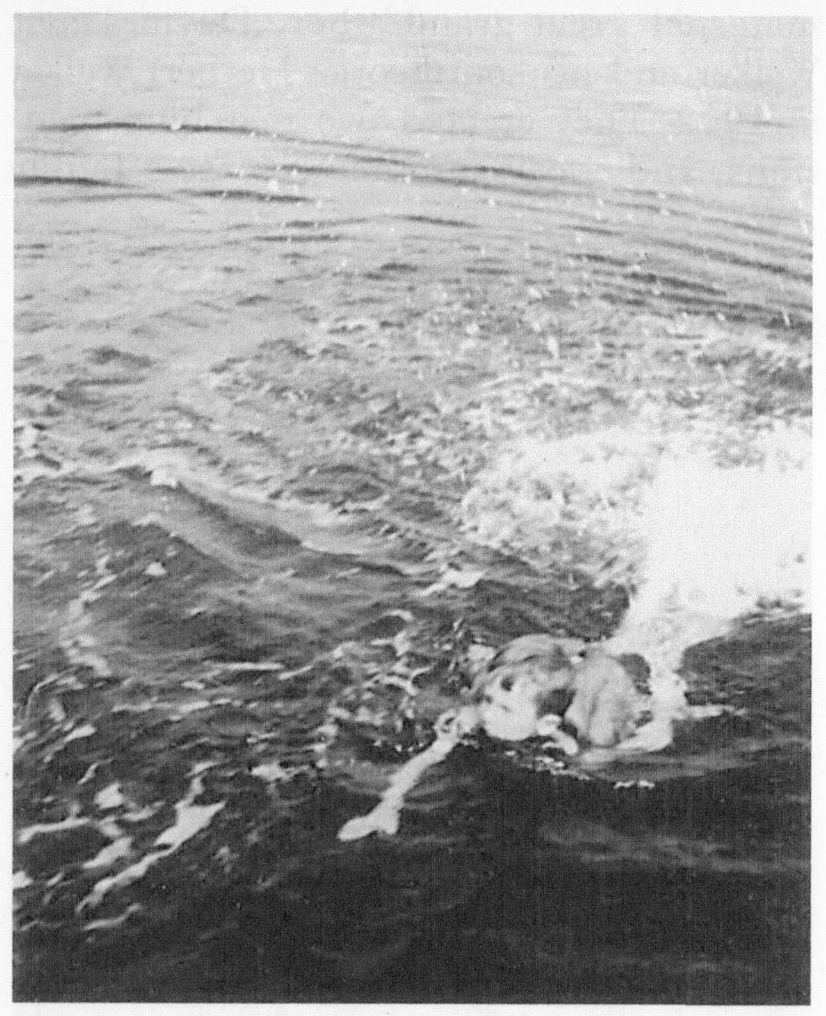

George swimming in the ocean.

— his father, mother, older brother Pres, younger sister Nancy, and younger brothers Jonathan and William ("Bucky") — would ride north to the summer retreat.

Tomboy was George's grandfather George Herbert Walker's lobster boat. The vessel was stored in Maine, and for those brief months, it was host to many maritime adventures. On board, George and Pres learned about driving a boat and navigating currents and tides and having a basic understanding of the local ocean floor. Especially in Maine waters, *Tomboy* was tested, its bow moving up and slamming down and its motor pushing it through the waves.

G. H. Walker also taught his grandsons how to fish. On calm days, he might cut the motor to rock on the surface. With "a basic green line wrapped around a wooden rack with cloth from an old shirt or handkerchief used as lure," they'd catch mackerel and pollock easily. The larger ones would put up a bit of a fight, but the prize was great: "Bringing one in, especially a green beauty, ranked right up there with eating ice cream and staying up late," recalled George.

By the ages of nine and eleven, George and Pres had proven to G. H. Walker they were capable of handling *Tomboy* on their own. From then on, they were almost always sea-bound; that's when George's passion for the sea and boats developed. "I loved the physical sensation of steering a powerful machine, throttle open in a following sea, and the surge that came when the waves lifted the stern and drove the bow down," he remembered.

When summer ended, the Bushes returned to their Victorian on Grove Lane in Greenwich, Connecticut, and to routine. In the morning, at the breakfast table, Prescott or Dorothy sat with their children and read from the Bible. Even when the kids were grown and out of the house, George's parents started their day this way. "Life gets so hectic that I feel I am constantly in a jet plane whirling through space. I am more determined than ever to let nothing interfere with our quiet little time for morning reading and prayer together each morning before [Prescott] goes to the Senate," Dorothy Walker Bush wrote to Anne Morrow Lindbergh after her book *Gift from the Sea* was published.

Beginning in first grade, George and Pres attended Greenwich Country Day School. George was a year too young, but his parents enrolled him so he and his brother could be together. The school was started by a group of local parents in 1925, and the founding principles were "studies, play, and character." The concept of the educational movement, which occurred in pockets across the suburban towns of the United States, was to prepare students for preparatory school by mimicking the curriculums.

There were plenty of extracurricular activities, such as marbles, which at Greenwich "dominated free time and after-school time." The tournaments "generated great excitement as marbles were won, lost, and traded with avarice." Classes were held in large estates around town, such as the Warner estate, which had a large tract of land for exploring, another important element of the school's mission. They attended classes through the fifth grade, and each day the boys would be dropped off by the family driver. After school, they'd scurry up the stairs of the Grove Lane house and turn right into the room they shared, closing the door behind them.

His briefcase in hand, Prescott took the train to New York City each day, where he worked at W. A. Harriman (which merged in 1931 to create Brown Brothers, Harriman and Company). At the age of twenty-two, Prescott served as Army field artillery captain during World War I. Having been described as "big, strong, principled," his children never wanted to do anything that warranted his disappointment or interference. Of course, occasionally they did. There was the time when George and Pres were eight and ten and paid a girl in the neighborhood to run across the living room naked. They never forgot running to her parents' house to apologize after their father heard what had happened. While his father "wasn't cozy like Mother," George remembered, he was warm to his children. In the 1930s, Prescott became more involved in politics, and volunteered as Greenwich's town moderator and later was elected to represent Connecticut in the U.S. Senate from 1951 to 1963. His father's career had an enormous influence on George, but his mother was his North Star.

"Dad taught us about duty and service. Mother taught us about dealing with life on a personal basis, relating to other people."

— GEORGE BUSH

George was especially close to his mother. She could do anything, and the tales of her competitive nature continue to be retold to new generations. There was the time she challenged a friend to swim from Walker's Point to the Kennebunk River Club, which was a mile away. "Thinking she was joking, the friend quit after a few hundred yards," but Dorothy, recalled George W. Bush, "swam the full distance in the frigid Atlantic waters." Tennis was her forte. In 1918, she

Dorothy and Prescott.

was one of eight to compete in the women's singles at the U.S. National Championships, which took place on the grass courts of Philadelphia Cricket Club in Pennsylvania. She raised her kids to be high achievers but above all humble.

George and Dorothy playing tennis.

Enough about yourself, George, she said to him during his 1980 campaign. "I pointed out that as a candidate, I was expected to tell voters something about my qualifications. She thought about that a moment, then reluctantly conceded. 'Well, I understand that, but try to restrain yourself.' "

When George's father Prescott ran for senate in 1950, Dorothy Walker Bush found herself in the unflattering limelight. She told *Connecticut Life* walking in a parade through the streets of New London behind a brass band was "ghastly." "She not only had no training for the goldfish bowl; she had been trained against it. Her father abhorred having his daughters photographed. Miss Porter's School in Farmington instilled in her the same distaste of publicity it gave Jacqueline Bouvier Kennedy a generation later," wrote *Connecticut Life* on May 4, 1961.

"[My mother] had these truisms that served me in good stead even when I got to be president of the United States. She said nobody likes a braggadocio. Don't be bragging about yourself all the time. Listen, don't talk all the time. She said give the other guy credit. She set a good example for all of us, and if we got hurt, she'd be there, to brush us off and get us back in the game."

— GEORGE BUSH

It is in the moments you are not trying to teach that your children learn, and Dorothy Walker Bush set the bar high. George envied and inherited by osmosis her competitive nature and her loyalty to family. Once he decided he liked Barbara Pierce from Rye, he made it his mission to woo her.

A Letter to My Future Children

In third grade, my class was asked to do a project on someone special in our lives. I chose my great-grandmother, Dorothy Walker Bush, who my mom "Doro" is named after. I asked Gampy if he could send me some information about his mom since I didn't know her very well. She passed away on my sixth birthday. Boy, did Gampy have a lot to say about his mum. Gampy gave me that gift, so I've decided to try and do the same for you about your great-grandfather, one of the greatest guys I know.

When people ask me about Gampy, it's hard for me to tell them how much he really means to me without getting emotional. Gampy is the kindest, most loving person I have ever known. You are lucky to have his genes.

Growing up, Gampy always put family first. My cousins and I couldn't have cared less about his job title — to us, he was our beloved Gampy. Sure, he was often dressed in nice suits and had lots of important meetings, but when the day was over he'd roll up his sleeves and drop down to the floor to play games with us. He made it a point to not bring his work home with him. When it was time to be with us, he was fully present.

One summer when I was about four, Gampy was president, and I was visiting up in Maine. I woke up in the middle of the night scared and padded down the steps of the Big House, through the kitchen and slipped into their dark bedroom. I tapped Gampy on the shoulder and whined something about the loud noises coming from outside my window. He reached out an arm, picked me up and placed me right in between him and Ganny. *Shh,* I remember him saying, *go to sleep.* I have never been happier than when I was wedged between them, always with the two dogs at the end of the bed. Gampy later recalled these nights (there were several) and said I was a "squirmy little thing." I must have kept them up, but they never let me know it.

Gampy has a thing for sayings. For example, his claim to fame — well, at least one of them — is that he was the first guy to say "You da Man!" Our family is still not sure if this one is totally true, but it has become one of his favorite sayings that he uses in his letters, especially when he wants to lift up someone. If Gampy tells you "you da man," he means it. Another one of his favorites that started during my Aunt Robin's short life is "love you more than tongue can tell." My cousins and I have heard this countless times from him, and every time is just as special.

Gampy was an athlete for most of his life and passed that competitive gene on to his children and grandchildren. He spent summers in Maine playing tennis, golf, speed boating, and running around with his grandchildren. Gampy kept up his tennis skills even into his later years. About ten years ago, he challenged each of his grandchildren to a tennis match — *mano a mano.* If you could beat Gampy, you won a crisp $100 bill. Folding green, as he liked to call it. As teenage kids and athletes ourselves, we thought this would be a sinch against our grandfather, who was in his eighties. We even felt kind of bad. Well, he easily defeated all of the grandkids who took him on. All except my cousin Ashley, who still beams about that win when asked about it today.

Gampy is and always has been so funny. He and Ganny have laughed their way through life together, and I believe that is a reflection of the strength of their marriage. Even through hard times, Gampy finds the humor. After his heartbreaking loss during the presidential election in 1992, Gampy, Ganny, and all of the staff who had worked tirelessly were defeated. Gampy invited

Dana Carvey, who famously imitated him throughout his presidency, to the White House to cheer everyone up.

When we visited Maine in the summer there were rules, which Ganny posted on the back of every door in the house. Bullet points such as: *Help Paula by picking up your towels and making your beds; throw away empty water bottles or soda cans; do your summer reading!* Ganny took on the role of "the Enforcer," whether she wanted to or not because Gampy just didn't have it in him to say no to his kids and grandkids. Enter the "Ranking Committee," which operated as follows:

"Gampy, can Marshall and I stay up and watch a movie past our bedtime?"

"I have to check with the Ranking Committee," he'd reply before disappearing. Then he'd come back and say that he was sorry but the Ranking Committee's answer was "no," so we'd have to go to bed on time.

We never knew who was on the Ranking Committee, but we always listened. Then years later, a photograph revealed the members: Gampy superimposed his head onto five different bodies. Mystery solved!

Gampy still makes us laugh with a funny face across the dinner table, or an unexpected burp — *Gotta get the poison out!* he says. Last summer, my mom, who also loves a good joke, brought a fart machine over to Ganny and Gampy's for dinner. Gampy was fascinated and pushed the button over and over. He finally let up so dinner could continue. We had all forgotten about the machine until Ganny announced she was heading to bed. She got up from her seat and made her way past Gampy toward the bedroom. Just as she walked by, he pressed the fart machine again. Perfect comedic timing even at ninety-three years old.

Another life lesson that Gampy instilled in us is to always put the other person first. In tough situations, our natural reaction is to think about how we are affected. But maybe the other person is suffering even more. His boat, *Fidelity,* was my grandfather's most prized material possession, of which he had very few. At twenty years old, my cousin Pierce was thrilled when Gampy invited him out on a trip on *Fidelity* and asked Pierce to dock the boat. This was Pierce's moment to shine. That particular day, though, the winds were blowing and after a couple of minutes battling the big waves and strong currents, he lost control and the boat washed ashore onto the rocks. The bottom of the boat was damaged. Pierce was devastated; he felt he had let our

Gampy down. To add insult to injury, Pierce borrowed our grandmother's car later that evening without asking. When he returned, Ganny wasn't happy. Pierce was in the doghouse and felt terrible. The next day, after a restless night, a note had been slipped onto Pierce's bed:

> Pierce —
> I remember the days when I felt I could do nothing right. But then the sun would come up and a bright new day would embrace me. Do not worry about the boat or the car incident. You are a good man who got a bad bounce, but all is well, believe me! I hate to see you worrying and down. You brighten my life, so forget yesterday and today's <u>little</u> incidents — you da man! And I love you. Ganny does, too.
>
> Gampy

Ten years later, this note means everything to Pierce, and he carries it on his phone with him to refer back to when things get tough.

Your great-grandfather has always had an uncanny ability to make everyone in his life from family and friends to new acquaintances feel special and loved — especially his bride.

Three: Courting

December 1941

On the night they met, Barbara mentioned to George that she'd be at a dance in Rye the next night. Poppy convinced his younger sister, Nancy, to join him and together they rounded up a few friends. When they arrived at the Apawamis Club, it didn't take long for Barbara and George to dance, but they were quickly interrupted. Jimmy, Barbara's older brother, was determined to build a roster for a basketball game. The Rye championship team was looking to challenge the local prep school boys to a match this Christmas break. Jimmy wanted to know — was George up for a little healthy competition?

Of course he was. In equal parts due to his competitive spirit and a deepening desire to see a certain someone in the stands. Yet, George got more of an audience than he or Barbara had anticipated. Her whole family had a suspicious interest in attending the pick-up game, and she guessed it wasn't to cheer on Jimmy.

The Rye boys won. After meeting Barbara's family, George took her out in his parents' Oldsmobile. The car choice for him was important: the Oldsmobile was the only family vehicle with a radio. Poppy was nervous they would "sit in stony silence and have nothing to say to one another," recalled Barbara.

It turns out they had a lot to talk about.

The conversation continued through letters when school vacation came to an end and she returned to Charleston, South Carolina, and he left for Andover, Massachusetts. In the early to mid-twentieth century, courting transpired through letters. The content was mostly brief, light, and fun, and, like dance partners, you might even have more than one special pen pal, but looping sentences together in cursive was how people stayed in touch and got to know one another. Written letters were also very revelatory, especially at first. Each envelope contained another handwritten clue directed at its recipient. Each timely reply, a confirmation of shared personal interest.

At Ashley Hall, Barbara had three roommates, and when the mail came they'd rip the paper envelopes to read. They might share a section or two from the letter, but Barbara kept most of hers close to her chest. "I was very immature, [George] really brought me up," she said, recalling their mail correspondence in her nineties. "He was mature because of the war and he always was more mature than I was."

In April of 1942, she seemed to have gained a bit more confidence and sent a flirtatious thinking-of-you postcard to George from Armonk, New York. Their vacations were overlapping for a day, and they planned to catch a movie with friends.

When the time came to pick a date for the Andover promenade George wrote Barbara, and she accepted. Each sentence of Barbara's letter is punctuated with a casual, cool humor.

She wasn't kidding about "knees knocking." Barbara was both excited and nervous at the invitation. She had never been kissed before, let alone attend a promenade as a boy's date. Two days after her seventeenth birthday, she was en route to Phillips Academy. Train cars full of seniors' dates arrived in Andover on June 10. Looking around, Barbara felt young compared to other dates

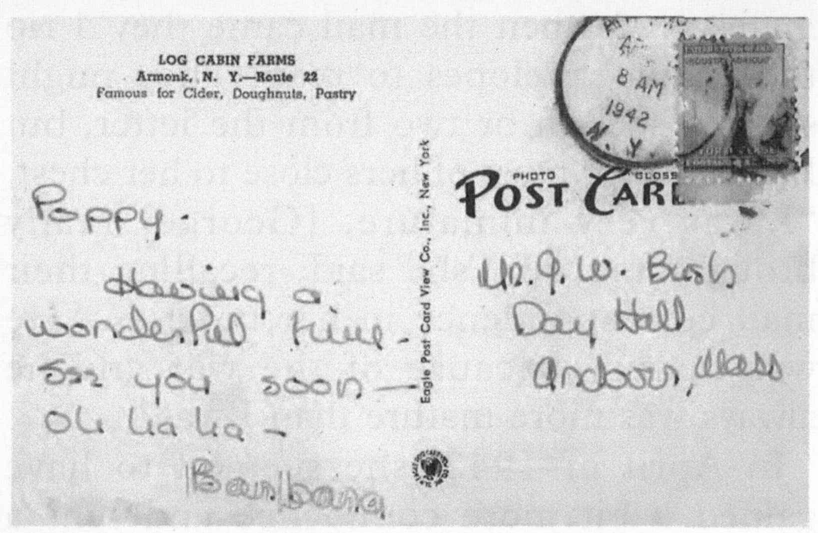

LOG CABIN FARMS
Armonk, N. Y.—Route 22
Famous for Cider, Doughnuts, Pastry
8 AM
1942
N. Y.
PHOTO
GLOSS
POST CAR
Eagle Post Card View Co., Inc., New York
Poppy -
Having a
wonderful time -
See you soon —
Oh la la -
Barbara
Mr. G. W. Bush
Day Hall
Andover, Mass

Postcard from Barbara to George, 1942.

who "obviously had been to a senior dance before."

George didn't seem to notice her hesitance; he was too eager to introduce Barbara Pierce to his friends and he took her all over campus. At 5 p.m. students and their guests had a Tea Dance in the Commons followed by dinner. Later, the promenade took place beneath streamers and balloons in the Borden Gymnasium.

Each student and his guest received a small white paper book with two lined pages, where they wrote in the names of the people they were to dance with. Like piecing together a well-negotiated puzzle, students figured out the order of dances before the event. Poppy had signed up a number of his friends to dance with Barbara, so she

Barbara Pierce · Ashley Hall · Charleston, S. C.

Friday-

Dear Poppy-

I think it was perfectly swell of you to invite me to the dance and I would love to come or go or whatever you say. I wrote mom yesterday or the day before and, rather logically, I haven't heard from her, BUT I'm sure she is going to let me come or go, etc. I really am excited, but scared to death, too. If you hear a big noise up there, don't worry, it's just my knees knocking.

Barbara's letter to George reads, "Dear Poppy, I think it was perfectly swell of you to invite me to the dance and I would love to come or go or whatever you say. I wrote mom yesterday or the day before, and rather logically, I haven't heard from her, BUT I'm sure she is going to let me come or go, etc. I really am excited, but scared to death, too. If you hear a big noise up there, don't worry, it's just my knees knocking."

wouldn't have to worry. The system, according to Barbara, was a way to make sure "you didn't go and get stuck with the person you went with."

Of course, George took the last dance. Afterward, they walked back to the house master's house where Barbara was staying. They chatted the whole way and when the walk and the evening were coming to an end, George leaned in for a kiss. "He kissed me on the cheek and I almost fainted," Barbara remembered in 2017. "I went in and — the poor girl who was rooming with me — I kept her awake all night telling her how wonderful he was."

Four:
Phillips Academy

> "The stranger who climbs to Andover Hill on any fine afternoon in June or October will see the broad playing fields dotted with little groups of boys, each absorbed in some outdoor sport."
>
> — PHILLIPS ACADEMY HEADMASTER, CLAUDE M. FUESS

"Poppy Bush Leads Team At Andover" read the headline of the torn newspaper clipping taped to a scrapbook. Beside the clipping are other reports of "Captain Bush" guiding the undefeated Andover soccer team. At Andover, athletics were nearly as important as academics, and to excel on the field meant a great deal to your character, perseverance, personal strength, and commitment. In his senior year, George was captain of the soccer and baseball teams as well as a member of the basketball team.

On the field, Poppy Bush was a star;

George (center), captain of the soccer team.

however, in the classroom things were different. He struggled through his studies in the first few years at Andover. His marks were low and his performance in the classroom was graded as average at best. It didn't help when in April of 1940, he became severely ill from a staph infection that caused his parents to withdraw him from school and bring him in for treatment at Massachusetts General Hospital. At the suggestion of a teacher, Poppy repeated a year at Andover, and he graduated in 1942 instead of 1941.

"It has been the ambition of the school to arouse in the undergraduates a love for games, not so much for the victory which may be won as for the pleasure of matching skill against skill, brawn against brawn. To this end there should be games of every sort, for the strong, for the agile, for the swift — even for the feeble and clumsy."

— PHILLIPS ACADEMY HEADMASTER, CLAUDE M. FUESS

That final year, he turned things around academically and graduated in the top quarter of his class. "That year was the making of George, a changing point," said his sister Nancy to her niece Dorothy years

George (front, fourth from left) and the baseball team, 1941.

George at his desk at Andover.

later. "It was a brush with death, brush number one. It was also his fifth year at Andover, where he was the great man — not the Great I Am, but he grew into this great leader on campus."

His time at the school allowed him to get to know his teachers and himself. He made friends easily with his amicable personality. When George made the decision to enlist, he received a letter of recommendation from Phillips Academy headmaster, Claude M. Fuess:

I understand that George Herbert Walker Bush, now a senior at Phillips Academy, Andover, and about to graduate on June 12, is an applicant for service in Naval Aviation, and I am very glad to give him my recommendation as a young man of high character, pleasing personality, and unquestioned loyalty. Mr. Bush has been a student at Phillips Academy under me for five years. He has maintained a uniformly high standing in his studies, and now stands well up in the top quarter of his class. In addition he has been very active in athletics, and this year has been the Captain of both the soccer and baseball teams, as well as a member of the basketball team. Furthermore, he has been a member of our Student Council for three years, and has taken quite unostentatiously a position of leadership in the undergraduate body. I regard him as one of the ablest boys I have ever known in this school, and can recommend him without reservation for any form of active naval, military, or aviation service.

George would eventually choose naval aviation, partially influenced by a trip to New York for Fleet Week, but to deploy seaward must have seemed like destiny given his love of the water, influenced by those sweet summers in Maine. In December 1941, his mind was made up. Now to find a person to get him through the dark days ahead.

FIVE:
BAR

Gooch's Beach wraps the coast of Kennebunkport. In the early morning hours, before beach goers have built their camps for the day, dogs run free. This is First Lady Barbara Bush's favorite routine. She follows the water's edge as it curves like a crescent moon, her dogs bounce beside her and Secret Service trails behind. For that reason, she's recognizable to most locals; however her signature style points her out, too — her large-brimmed hat shades her face, and she's always dressed in color.

In 2017, she was having trouble breathing, and had yet to make it over to the sandy stretch. "My dream is to walk on that beach once more this summer," she said at the age of ninety-two. "I'm going to do it, I've got to do it. I have a lot of friends I haven't seen."

Friends of both the human and canine types. She knows the names of pets and owners who also walk in the mornings between May and October when she's in town. Twice the town attempted to ban dogs from the beach during certain hours, and twice she wrote a letter defending the tradition. The town decided the dogs could stay.

Her love of dogs is her other signature. Her famous canines, C. Fred and Millie, both penned children's books — *C. Fred's Story* and *Millie's Book.* Millie had puppies during her first year in the White House, which overjoyed the public. One puppy stayed (Ranger became President Bush's dog) and the others were adopted, including Pickles, who went to Will and Sarah Farish's farm in Versailles, Kentucky. When the Queen of England was visiting the farm, she took a photograph with the pup, and gave the image to Barbara as a gift when she hosted her at a luncheon at Buckingham Palace.

After Millie's puppies were born, a few press conferences were held in their honor. Newscasters asked playful questions and filmed the dogs clumsily climbing over one another and tripping over their short legs. Barbara stood behind the pen laughing at the tiny creatures. "It's just a constant source of pleasure watching them," she smiled down.

Dogs have always brought her joy, even as a little girl.

Barbara Pierce grew up in Rye, New York, which is a town away from the Connecticut border and just over thirty miles to New York City. Barbara's parents moved there with her two older siblings, Jimmy and Martha, before she was born on June 8, 1925. Barbara remained the baby of the family until her little brother Scott was born when she was five years old.

Her childhood home was a brick, three-story house on Onondaga Street, smack in the middle of a neighborhood of kids. A tree house occupied a big maple tree and in the summer the yard was perfumed as her mother's gardens bloomed.

The home was within walking distance to Rye Country Day, which Barbara attended from seventh through ninth grade. Her father also walked fifteen minutes each morning to catch the train to Manhattan, and sometimes Barbara walked with him. "Some of my happiest memories were walking with Daddy to the station in the morning," she recalled. In later years, she and George discovered their fathers commuted on the same train. Who knows if they had sat next to one another reading the morning paper or playing bridge in the Club Car after work.

> "[My father] was the fairest man I knew until I met George Bush."
> — BARBARA BUSH

Barbara described her father as a "smiling man" who was close to six feet tall. He grew up in Dayton, Ohio, where he was a star athlete. He played football, basketball, tennis, and baseball at Miami University of

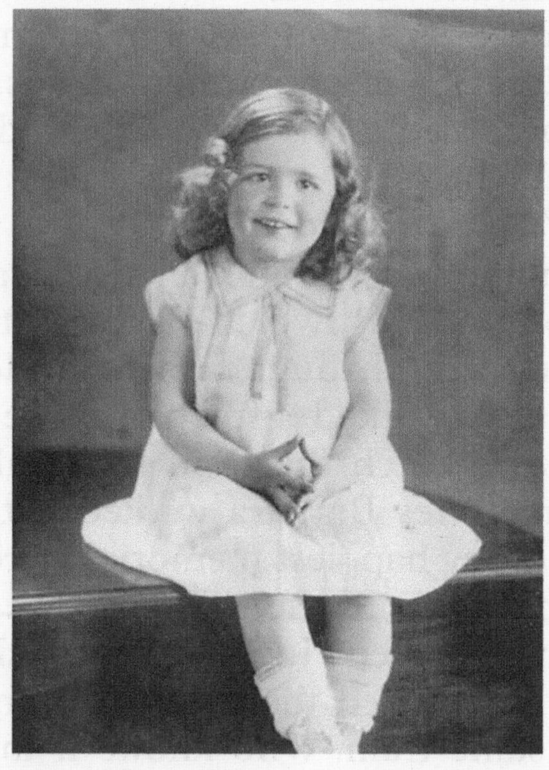

Barbara as a young girl.

Young Barbara wearing her signature pearls.

Ohio. At one legendary football game in 1913, Miami beat Denison 19–0 and "Monk" (as he was known to teammates) had four field goals, a touchdown and an extra-point, accounting for all 19 points. In 1968, years after graduating, he became the first M man, an honor for the most talented players, and in 1972, he was inducted into the university's Hall of Fame.

Off the field, the jock had his eye on the girl he believed to be the prettiest in Oxford

Family portrait of Marvin and Pauline Pierce and their children, with Barbara on Pauline's lap.

Female College down the street, and he just had to have her. "They started dating and that was it," recalled Barbara's brother Scott in his late eighties. "Pierce men don't tend to stray. They can't handle rejection, so when they find a woman they hold on to her desperately." Before taking off for the war in 1918, he proposed and she accepted.

She was Pauline Robinson. She grew up in Marysville, Ohio, and was the daughter of Lulu and James Robinson, a lawyer who served on Ohio's Supreme Court. She loved her garden. Pauline was so dedicated to her plants that in the colder months, she reared earthworms in the basement, which made the soil of her gardens all the richer. She hated starlings, which chased the other birds from her feeders, so she paid Scott twenty-five cents for every starling he shot with his BB gun. She was absorbed in banishing weeds, trimming, and watering, and she would eventually take her talents to serve as the conservation chairman on the Garden Club of America. When Barbara would come home from playing in the warmer months, her mother would be bent over her flowers and covered head to toe for protection from the sun. "Everything was more beautiful because of my mother," said Barbara.

On Fridays, Barbara and her mother went to dance lessons at Miss Covington's Dance School. All the mothers watched from the balcony of the Episcopal Church and all the mothers wore hats — except Pauline Pierce. "In Rye, New York, you had a hat on at dancing school and it always embarrassed me that my mother didn't wear a hat," she said. Other things worried Barbara, too, like getting picked last to dance. When too many boys were huddled in the bathroom, or just found other ways to skip the weekly chore, Miss Covington would ask for volunteers to lead. Measuring taller, and slightly wider, than most, and feeling awkward in her silk dress, young Barbara shot her hand in the air. "That way I avoided being the last girl chosen or rejected altogether," she remembered. "Finally Mother absolutely forbade me to raise my hand again."

Barbara's relationship with her mother was strained. Then when her younger brother Scott was born, Barbara felt ignored. He occupied all their mother's attention, not just because he was the baby but because he was sick. After he fell off his older brother's bike, Xrays revealed a cyst in his arm. From the age of two until he was nine, Scott was in and out of the hospital, and would sometimes stay for months at a time. "That made me the darling of my mother's eye, but I'm sure that was a pain in the neck to my sister," said Scott.

Barbara longed for her mother's affection and attention, but it never came. Pauline was consumed by housework, clubs and committees and her youngest; she left little time for her third child. Barbara would often hear her mother mumbling about "when her ship came in," as if she never was where she wanted to be. As she matured, Barbara became overly cautious of the traits she didn't wish to adopt from her mother, and she made a personal pledge to try to be grateful and make the most of her given situation.

> "You have two choices in life: You can like what you do, or you can dislike it. I have chosen to like it."
>
> — BARBARA BUSH

In 1921, Marvin Pierce took a job as the assistant to the president at McCall's, which produced women's magazines such as *McCall's Magazine* and *Redbook.* He became president of the company in 1947.

The pulp magazine was targeted at housewives, but it was filled with goodies for younger girls, too. There were coveted paper dolls, which children could cut out and collect. Occasionally Barbara's father would come home with the pattern books, and she and her neighborhood friends would play for hours, imagining families and slipping them into paper outfits.

While the Pierces were fiscally conservative during the Depression, they were well off enough to still have someone to help with the laundry and ironing as well as a cook, who lived on the third floor. Family dinner was an evening tradition. Barbara remembers the nights they'd have graham crackers and cream for dinner — a delicious, but far from leafy dish. While Marvin went in for seconds, Pauline was watchful of her daughters' figures. "Eat up, Martha. Not you, Barbara!" was her not-so-subtle jab.

Martha was a beauty. She modeled for *Vogue* magazine and even got on the cover in August 1940 for the college fashion issue. Pauline and Martha got along so well that Marvin went a little further out of his way to show Barbara love. "Because she was the great beauty and mother adored her and they got along and they shopped and I didn't do any of those things, Daddy took care of me," said Barbara.

Differences aside, Barbara followed in the footsteps of her sister, who was five years older. They attended the same schools and even dated boys in the same circles, and by tenth grade, Barbara left Rye, like her sister, to attend Ashley Hall in Charleston, South Carolina. When she arrived, the school felt very far from home. In the Southern heat, large trees draped in Spanish moss grew out of the soft earth. The campus was clothed in gardens, studded with fountains and surrounded by marsh, creeks, and forests. Exotic plants and refined Victorian buildings were left over from the estate's series of extravagant occupants.

Founder Mary Vardrine McBee still ran the school when Barbara attended. She opened Ashley Hall in 1909. The mission was to "produce an educated woman who is independent, ethically responsible, and prepared to meet the challenges of society with confidence." Until graduation, however, they were under careful watch. "Gloves and hats had to be worn if the girls were leaving the campus and a chaperone was never far behind," writes Ileana Strauch in her book *Ashley Hall.*

"Pearls and Amethyst"

We wear the pearls for whiteness
Of friendship's sacred tryst.
The future's mystic
Is veiled in amethyst.
But rarer is the token
The light reveals to all —
The golden links unbroken
Speak of Ashley Hall.

"In an Oak-Shaded Garden"

In an oak-shaded garden
In a city by the sea.
There stands old Ashley Hall, so dear,

There's where I love to be.
In days of mirth and sadness, too,
She stands serene and calm,
A beacon bright to lead us on,
And keep us from all harm.
Chorus: Oh, Ashley Hall, dear Ashley Hall,
That's where I love to be.

There were perks, too, for the school located on 172 Rutledge Avenue — dances with local boys' schools, Porter Military Academy and the Citadel, where sodas were sold and records were played. For older girls, the Shell House became a smoking lounge reserved for seniors and faculty. If a younger girl was caught in the building "uninvited" then she would be "forced to bake cookies for the seniors and give a sincere apology to the senior class during chapel." Life inside the wrought-iron gates was innocent and insular, but that shifted in Barbara's first year.

When the United States declared war, the girls at Ashley Hall pitched in where possible. The class of 1943 did not publish a yearbook or an annual issue of the school magazine, *Cerberus,* to conserve paper. Outside the Fort Sumter Hotel, which was being used as a naval headquarters, students volunteered on a YMCA tea car.

"The war changed everything."
— BARBARA BUSH

Everyone was encouraged to do their part. *McCall*'s February 1942 issue featured a woman on the cover and affixed to her white collar was a pin with the words "I've enlisted" on it below a white star. So many men around the country were enlisting, *McCall*'s created a place for women to do the same.

"Although the scrupulous observance of your responsibilities as housewives may not seem a dramatic means of expressing

Barbara with her friends.

Barbara and friends taking a break from their studies.

your will to serve, be certain of this: your men — your sons, your husbands, your sweethearts — are only as secure as you make them. The uniforms they wear, the food they eat, the equipment they carry, the arms they employ to strike at the heart of the enemy all come out of your day-to-day living."

— *MCCALL'S,* FEBRUARY 1942

Inside readers could sign a pledge to buy carefully, take good care of the things they have, and waste nothing. "McCall's will send to every signer of this pledge a certificate of honor, testifying that your name is on file in our national capital. And, as long as the supply lasts, McCall's will also send to each signer a red, white, and blue emblem, symbolic of your enlistment in this struggle for victory by the people of the United States. ENLIST NOW!"

Restrictions on the home front included rationing of food and gas, and drives were set up to collect important wartime materi-

Barbara's graduating class at Ashley Hall. She is in the top row, fifth from left.

als such as metal, rubber, nylon, and paper. Since trains and airplanes were reserved for soldiers, personal travel was deemed "unpatriotic." Therefore the Pierce family did not attend Barbara's high school graduation in the spring of 1943. In her traditional white dress, Barbara walked across the stage to receive her diploma carrying a bouquet of flowers. She was ready to head home for the summer to prepare for her freshman year at Smith.

Of course, she also made arrangements to spend time with a certain soldier in training who had been occupying most of her thoughts.

I like to think I have a special relationship with my grandmother, but I know there are lots of people out there who feel the same way. Ganny values her family and friends and over the years has created long lasting and loving relationships with countless people. But I'm going to use this space to tell you about my relationship with Ganny and what she means to me.

The earliest story around our relationship is just a few months after I was born. Our little family — my mom, my dad, my brother Sam, and me — lived in Cape Elizabeth, Maine, just outside of Portland. Apparently I cried through the night for the first several months of my life. By the time my mom brought me to Kennebunkport for the weekend to visit my grandparents, she and my poor dad were exhausted. When we arrived at Walker's Point my mom nearly collapsed into my grandmother's arms when she greeted us at the door. My grandmother ordered my mom to go to sleep right away, she would take care of me. Sixteen glorious hours later, my mom woke up and came running to my grandparents' room. *Why did they let her sleep so long? Didn't Ellie have to eat?* My grandmother looked at her. "Oh please, don't be silly. Paula ran to the store and picked up some formula." That was it, no more breastfeeding for me! She taught me independence at four months old.

I admired my grandmother so much as a little girl. I remember her vividly during their time at the White House. My mom, brother, and I lived in the D.C. area and would visit often. I remember sitting in her closet, looking through her dresses and shoes and opening up her drawer filled with her signature pearls. I'd try on her shoes and pearls and walk around pretending I was First Lady. In third grade, when my class was asked to do a report on someone they admire, I chose my grandmother. I dressed up in a purple dress, borrowed some of her pearls, and carried a stuffed animal springer spaniel dog with me to school. My mom helped me curl my hair. I remember being so proud to be Ganny that day.

Ganny was the rule maker when we were growing up. Not that she desired to but she was married to George Bush, who couldn't say no to his grandkids. Someone had to do the job! One of the most classic Ganny stories involved my little brother Robert. At Ganny and Gampy's house, Klondike bars were always (and still are) in the freezer. They are the perfect dessert to offer up to lunch or dinner guests. My brother Robert took a strong liking to the Klondike bars and would often be caught red-handed sneaking them when he shouldn't be. Ganny finally had enough after catching him sneaking in at breakfast time. Without telling anyone, Ganny padlocked the freezer shut, and it could only be opened with a key and code. You can imagine Robert's disappointment the next time he went for a treat.

Even at ninety-two, she was sharper than a razor's edge. I credit her sharp mind to her voracious love of reading, needlepointing, and letter writing. She also loves to talk. Popping in for a quick visit with Ganny can turn into an hour or two; she loves to chat about the goings on in the world or in our family. Almost every morning during the summer in Maine, my mom and Ganny get together in their bathrobes, coffee in hand, and talk. Sometimes my uncles join depending on when they are in town. I've forced myself out of bed a few times for this (it's at 6 a.m., mind you!), and I am always glad when I do. There is something so special about coming together when the sun is still rising over the ocean, and everyone else is still sleeping.

The most obvious characteristic about Ganny, whether you've known her a long time or just meet her for the first time, is her deep love and protection of Gampy. Don't mess with George Bush because Barbara Bush will come after you! She is his biggest supporter in everything that he has done in his career and life. She has stood by his side through countless trips, speeches, rallies, debates, and social events. She has cheered him on in tennis matches, hung on to his arm while his boat, *Fidelity,* barreled through the Atlantic Ocean at 65 mph, and has defended him to anyone who has ever said a bad word about him.

Six: "I'm Going In."

"At first, to the American sailors at Pearl, the hum of engines sounded routine, and why not? To them, the idea of war seemed palpable but remote. And then, in one horrible instant, they froze in disbelief. The abstract threat was suddenly real. But these men did not panic. They raced to their stations, and some strapped pistols over pajamas, and fought and died. And what lived was the shock wave that soon swept across America, forever immortalizing December 7th, 1941."

— PRESIDENT GEORGE H. W. BUSH SPEAKING AT PEARL HARBOR ON DECEMBER 7, 1991

When a traumatic event occurs that rattles your life, changing who you are and how you view the world, most people can remember everything about that exact moment. The news of Pearl Harbor rattled a nation and shot across America as young George Bush was walking across the green at Phillips Academy. "My thoughts in those days didn't turn to world events, but mainly to simpler things, more mundane things like making the basketball team, entering college. That walk across the campus marked an end of innocence for me," remembered George during his speech at Pearl Harbor on December 7, 1991.

Young George didn't want to sit on the sidelines. He was overcome with emotion and his immediate reaction was to enlist as soon as possible. "Like most people in the country, I wanted to participate, I wanted to go fight for my country," he later recalled.

Six months after Pearl Harbor, on June 12, 1942, George turned eighteen, graduated, and enlisted all in the same day. Secretary of War Henry L. Stimson delivered Phillips Academy's commencement speech. "[He] advised my class to go to college. He predicted it would be a long war, and there would be plenty of time for us to serve," remembered George. In the audience for his graduation, George's father hoped his son would consider Stimson's words. He was so young and would have plenty of time to fight. After the ceremony, Prescott looked his second oldest in the eyes to get an answer.

"George — did the Secretary say anything to change your mind?"

George looked up at his father confidently. "No, sir. I'm going in."

Prescott nodded and shook his son's hand. Not wasting any time, George drove to Boston to enlist. By September 1942, he was bound for basic training in Chapel Hill, North Carolina. "My father took me down to Pennsylvania Station in New York. [That] great big guy put his arm around me and that was the first time I ever saw him shed a tear," remembered George, who climbed aboard a train not knowing any of the fellow passengers.

The summer George left for training, everything was happening quickly, including his courtship with Barbara. Before leaving for North Carolina, George sealed his relationship with Barbara by delivering a real kiss on the lips — a first for both of them. Months later, after his mother caught his younger sister "kissing a beau," she wrote George while he was stationed at Chapel Hill, inquiring about affection before marriage — *was it proper?* George confessed to a kiss he did not regret.

Now about your question, Mum. I do love

to kid you and did this summer but I agree with you in part. I would hate to have Nancy a necker at heart. Nothing could be worse. Kissing is not an obligation a girl owes a boy regardless of how often he takes her out or how much he spends . . . but I don't think that it is entirely wrong for a girl to be kissed by a boy. Let us take this famous case Pierce vs. Bush summer '42. I kissed Barbara and am glad of it. I'd tell you, Mrs. Pierce, or anybody, but at the same time I might as well tell you I have never felt towards another girl as I do towards her. Whether the feeling is mutual I cannot say. To get back to my example, however, if Barbara sort of forgets me, which is not unlikely, as I have no chance to see her at all. I don't believe she will ever dislike me more for having kissed her. She knows how I felt towards her and she must have shared some of the same feeling or she would not have allowed me to kiss her. I have never kissed another girl. . . .

George and his mother discussed many topics through letters. In hasty cursive, he told her about his soccer games. In letters that he didn't have much news to report, he blended mundane details about showering

George in Navy uniform.

and marching, then he'd apologize for not having anything new to say. He scribbled drawings of what he was learning in flight school. At the bottom of his letters, his words became large and loose, as if his mind was already on to the next thing on his list.

They even discussed more serious topics, like sex before marriage. Some men and women who were uncertain of their fates decided to skip the long-established rule of waiting until marriage, but George and his older brother Prescott did not agree.

> For a kiss to mean engagement is a very beautiful idea, Mama, but it went out a while back I guess. Now for me to continue and tell you the facts of life — of the life I'm living in the [1940s] — Apparently Mum you seemed so terribly surprised when Pressy and I hinted around about the 'things that went on'? Pressy and I share a view, which very few others even in Greenwich share. That's regarding intercourse before marriage. I would hate to find that my wife had known some other man, and it seems to me only fair to her that she be able to expect the same standards from me. Pres agrees as I said before, but now many others our age will. Daddy has never discussed such things with us — of this I am very glad. But we have learned as the years went on by his character what is right and what is wrong.

George and Barbara exchanged letters, too, and when she left for her senior year at

Ashley Hall, she stopped to see George in North Carolina. Before she got on the train, George had a request: "He wrote and asked me to please tell everyone I was eighteen years old. He was the youngest man in flight training school and got teased all the time." While Barbara had prepared for the exchange before arriving — memorizing her new date of birth and practicing out loud — no one on campus seemed to care. "Do you know how many people asked me how old I was? Zero!" she said.

> Dear Mum,
> Well today sure was wonderful . . . I met Barbara at the Inn at 12. She took a cab over from Raleigh. She looked too cute for words — really beautiful. We had a sandwich in town and then walked. I showed her the plant and then we walked over to Keenan Stadium. When we started it was clear, but once there it poured — just buckets. We got some protection from the canvas covered press box, but couldn't leave there . . . Not thrilling but such fun just seeing her. We laughed at everything. I had formulation at six so we went back to the Inn. She took a bus for Raleigh where she is staying overnight with a girl from school.

She was so swell to come way over here. I sure am glad you said "grand idea" to Mrs. Pierce.

Much love to all,
Pop

When George moved on to training at the frozen airfields of Wold-Chamberlain Naval Air Station in Minneapolis, Minnesota, in November 1942, he continued to be self-conscious about his age. "They all ask my age and with a perfectly straight face I say, nineteen," he wrote to his mom. He also tried to pass the story on to her, but in some cases it was too late. "Everyone here thinks I'm 19 and still I'm by far the youngest," he wrote his mom on November 25, 1942. "So if anyone asks who might see me while in the Navy, it's 'George and he's 19.' I suppose you told Winfield's Ma I was just 18, too! I hope not." Perhaps exacerbating the situation, George asked Pauline Pierce to send him a photograph of Barbara. Down at school in South Carolina, Barbara didn't have anything to send him, but her mother's choice wasn't what Barbara had in mind. "She sent him one that was several years old and featured my cairn puppy, Sandy. Poor Poppy. That picture made it look like he was dating a twelve-year-old," remembered Barbara. "Shortly afterward, I had a graduation picture taken and at least it was without the dog."

That same year, George was away for the first time for Thanksgiving and Christmas. His parents sent him a bracelet, goggles, and a bathrobe. Barbara sent him argyle socks she stitched herself, which he wrote his mom, "were far better than I expected — really pretty darn good!" The Pierces sent him a big box of food. His distance from home, the weight of the missions he trained for, and the new men he was bunking with from all over the country really impacted George. He may have stretched his age, but he had already grown up.

> Thanksgiving comes tomorrow. I guess that I will hardly notice it here — that is outwardly as we can't leave the base and just get 1 hour off, but it won't just be a regular day, Mum. We all do have some-things to be thankful for, even though the days are darker than when we could all be together. I guess I'm the most thanks-giving fellow here because even though I'm a couple of thousand miles off I'm lucky, Mum. Lucky for you and Dad and all the family and so many other things. I thought when I was away

at school I understood it all, but being away in the Navy for this long and with so many different types of fellows has made me see more clearly still how much I do have to be thankful for. Though I'm now away and will be for a long time to come, I don't feel lost and I don't feel left out of a thing. I miss you very much — yes, that's true, but tomorrow I can think with pleasure of you all at home and I can say to myself — that's what I have to be thankful for.

Much love, Mum dear!

Pop

No matter how much he matured, the colorless landscape of Minnesota and the intensity of his training seemed to elicit the gravity of the missions ahead. The teenager struggled with the task ahead of him to fight and kill. On Thanksgiving he wrote home: "It's days like this that makes me anxious to be out fighting — though I know I can never become a killer, I will never feel right until I have actually fought. Being physically able and young enough I belong out at the front and the sooner there, the better. The job seems so tremendous, yet it must end and when it does and we have won perhaps days like this will once again be

George's graduating flight class.

symbolic of happiness and freedom and the ironic note added by a brutal war will be far removed . . ."

After passing his training in North Carolina and Minnesota, George traveled south to the Naval Air Station in Corpus Christi, Texas. He and Barbara continued to exchange letters, but she kept him guessing a little bit. Sometimes her true feelings were confirmed through a third party. He was a boy in love: eager, frenetic, and occasionally frustrated.

> I got a letter from F. Von Stade. He was on a 14 day furlough at Aiken recovering from pneumonia — what a break. Anyway he called up Barbara . . . He claims Barbara said she was glad I was in Texas where the girls are lousy so maybe I'm still in. I sure do hope so. If she 'fluffed me off' without warning I would be absolutely sick no kidding. Every day practically guys are getting 'fluffed off' from girls they've left . . . All the time it happens. You know Mum it's funny being thrown in with a bunch of guys so much older — They don't seem older, but here they are, all thinking and talking about getting married etc. Everyone asks me, after looking at Barbara's

picture, when I'm going to marry her. Good [heavens]! To think that last year at this time I was thinking along lines of prep school proms and stuff seems unbelievable . . . I do still love (I honestly

George readies for a flight.

feel sure of it) Barbara, Mum, yet I know that there is such a chance of her meeting some other guy. She is so very young and so darn attractive and I could hardly expect her to keep caring about me for years. ENOUGH OF THIS!!!!! You both must think I'm crazy!

Much love,
Pop

On June 9, 1943, George received his Navy wings and became the youngest officer in the U.S. Naval Reserve. George's training was intense and also isolated him from his world of family, friends, and Barbara. With limited contact with her, he worried she would get bored of the distance and leave him for someone else. When Barbara didn't respond to George for over three weeks, he wrote his mother about his anguish: "Mum, I'm really worried. I hope it's one of her lapses which she falls in occasionally either because she's busy or just to keep me anxious and interested; but I haven't gotten but 1 letter in 3 1/2 weeks. Before, there were a couple of 2 week famines but never this. I don't know, I hope it's not the 'fluff.' "

George in the cockpit.

SEVEN: SECRET'S SAFE

Whatever the reason for Barbara's stalled replies, it was not the "fluff." She was wild about Poppy Bush and everyone knew it. George was due home for seventeen days before he had to report to the U.S. naval air station in Fort Lauderdale, Florida.

Somehow Dorothy Bush picked up on all of this, as mothers do, and she invited Barbara to Kennebunkport that summer to meet the family. "I guess Mrs. Bush had all sorts of reasons to invite me, but I suspect they wanted to see as much of their son as possible before he went off to war," she recalled. With Barbara there in Maine, George wouldn't be anxious to get back to Rye, New York, every weekend. "That was my first trip to Kennebunkport, Maine, and my first glimpse of our beloved Walker's Point."

On the train ride north, George beamed. He talked about everyone she'd meet and told her stories about them. In Barbara's mind everyone seemed too good to be true. She was intimidated by his close family, and his older siblings, aunts, and uncles who were there with their spouses.

The Walkers and Bushes welcomed George's new friend, of course, but not without a healthy dose of teasing. The family had a horse-drawn wagon and it just so happened that the horse's name was Barsil. "George's brother Pres used to tease me and call me Barsil," recalled Barbara. "That is how I got my nickname, Bar."

Jonathan remembered going sailing with the two lovebirds. George was really good at making Barbara laugh but didn't seem to pay attention to much else. "George invariably wanted to go sailing, but once we got on the boat he would just stretch out and go on kidding Barbara while I did the actual sailing and Barbara rubbed George's back," Jonathan told author Joe Hyams many years later.

Aside from playful jokes and new nicknames, the war loomed and their time together waned. They spent each minute together: soaking in the summer days with picnics, bike riding, swimming, beachcombing, talking as they watched the sun sink and the moon rise up from the horizon.

George couldn't take his eyes off of Barbara and she couldn't stop smiling.

On that trip, they both confirmed their feelings for one another and made a promise to get married. It wasn't a formal engagement because George didn't have a ring to present, but it was their shared secret that would fill them with hope through the next few months.

> One last thing, sweet Mama! The way you and Dad both were so wonderful about Barbara probably meant more to me than anything. After all you hadn't seen me in ages and yet you didn't object to my running off. I needn't bother to tell you how much Barbara means to me — pretty evident I guess — knowing this you must know how happy you made me by being so marvelous about having her up etc.
>
> Goodnight and much much love,
>
> Pop

Eight: Secret's Out

The secret didn't last long. A classmate at Smith kept pressing Barbara to go out on a double date. After Barbara declined a few times, the classmate decided she must not like men and said she was an item with her roommate, Margie. That's when Margie told everyone Barbara was actually engaged to George Bush.

George and Barbara had to announce their engagement to their friends and families, and they were both relieved to do so. George wrote home to his mother: "I'm glad I told you about Bar & me. You probably knew already; but do tell Dad!" He had written weeks earlier confident in his affection despite his young age. "I'm just so convinced that Barbara is <u>the</u> girl for me."

Dorothy witnessed their obvious affection at Walker's Point and wrote to Barbara that fall: "I have felt all along so grateful, so very grateful, that Pop should have lost his heart to such as lovely person as Barbara Pierce . . . If I must be honest I must confess that your confession did not surprise me as all I had to do in Maine was to see you looking at each other to read right in your eyes how you both felt."

At the ages of eighteen and nineteen, they were promised to be married. It is young now, and it was young then, but so much had changed because of the war. "I was so young it was amazing," remembered Barbara. "You would never have allowed your children to get engaged at that age if it hadn't been that they knew he was going overseas. . . . Of course, his parents would have said anything to make him happy and mine just wanted to get rid of me I guess."

Dearest Barbara,
Mr. Bush and I wanted to send you this token of our affection, on this very important day in our lives.

We are so happy Barbara, and feel so special, blessed, that you should be coming into our family — Had Pops searched the world he couldn't have found anyone who would have pleased us as well.

With so much to live for, he just has to come back safely, and I am sure he will.

Thank you my dear for making him and all of us so happy. God bless you both.

Affectionately, Dotty W. Bush

Dear Barb,

Mother telephoned you this morning while I was . . . downstairs and told me nothing about her intentions. Therefore I am writing you this note in lieu of telling you over the phone how happy I am for you in your choice of a future husband. He is a swell guy and you'll always be happy with him come hell or high water. I don't know what mother said but as for me I accept your decision without any conditions other than those that you imposed upon yourselves in your letter. All we can do is to give you the advantages, which we have found to lie in honesty and integrity and just plain common decency and from that base let you steer your own course. You have done well, Barb, so far and may God keep you and Poppy happy no matter how rough the going. May He also bring him back safely from this job immediately ahead of him.

All my love,
Dad

Barbara submitted a formal wedding announcement to the *New York Times* on December 12, 1943. George received a copy and ripped it out to fold into his wallet. He wanted to keep it close to him. He kept that page for decades, torn and yellowed, what's left of the pulp is now part of the George Bush Presidential Library and Museum's collection.

December 12, 1943

My Darling Bar,
This should be a very easy letter to write — words should come easily and in short it should be simple for me to tell you how desperately happy I was to open the paper and see the announcement of our engagement, but somehow I can't possible say all in a letter I should like to.

I love you, precious, with all my heart and to know that you love me means my life. How often I have thought about the immeasurable joy that will be ours some day. How lucky our children will be to have a mother like you —

MISS BARBARA PIERCE, daughter of Mr. and Mrs. Marvin Pierce of Rye, N. Y., will marry Ensign George Herbert Walker Bush, Naval Air Corps, son of Mr. and Mrs. Prescott S. Bush of Greenwich, Conn. Miss Pierce was graduated from Ashley Hall, Charleston, S. C., and is a student at Smith college, Northampton, Mass. Her father is executive vice president of McCall corporation. Mr. and Mrs. Scott Pierce of Radcliffe road and Mrs. James E. Robinson of Columbus and the late Judge Robinson are her grandparents. Ensign Bush, an alumnus of Phillips Exeter academy at Andover, Mass., received his wings in June at Corpus Christi, Tex. He is a grandson of Mr. and Mrs. George Herbert Walker of New York and of Samuel Prescott Bush of Columbus and the nephew of Maj. and Mrs. James Smith Bush of Dayton and of Capt. and Mrs. G. H. Walker Jr. of

The wedding announcement from the New York Times.

As the days go by time of our departure draws nearer. For a long time I had anxiously looked forward to the day when we would go abroad and set to sea. It seemed that obtaining that goal would be all I could desire for some time, but, Bar, you have changed all that. I cannot say that I do not want to go — for that would be a lie. We have been working for a long time with a single purpose in mind, to be so equipped that we could meet and defeat our enemy. I do want to go because it is my part, but now leaving presents itself not as an adventure but as a job which I hope will be over before long. Even now, with a good while between us and the sea, I am thinking of getting back. This may sound melodramatic, but if it does it is only my inadequacy to say what I mean. Bar, you have made my life full of everything I could ever dream of — my complete happiness should be a token of my love for you.

Wednesday is definitely the commissioning and I do hope you'll be there. I'll call Mum tomorrow about my plan. A lot of fellows put down their parents or wives and they aren't going so you could pass as a Mrs. — Just say you lost the invite and give your name. They'll check the list and you'll be in. How proud I'll be if you can come.

I'll tell you all about the latest flying developments later. We have so much to do and so little time to do it in. It is frightening at times. The seriousness of this thing is beginning to strike home. I have been made asst. gunnery officer and when Lt. Houle leaves I will be gunner officer. I'm afraid I know very little about it but [I] am excited at having such a job. I'll tell you all about this later too.

The wind of late has been blowing like mad and our flying has been cut to a minimum. My plane, #2 now, is up at Quonset, having a camera installed. It is Bar #2 but purely in spirit since the Atlantic fleet won't let us have names on our planes.

Goodnight, my beautiful. Everytime I say beautiful you about kill me but you'll have to accept it —

I hope I get Thursday off — there's still a chance.

Barbara did attend the commissioning of the *San Jacinto* on December 15, 1943, at the Philadelphia Naval Yard. She traveled with Dorothy Bush who carried a precious object — her sister Nancy's ring. Before the ceremony began, George presented Barbara with the star sapphire engagement ring that glowed a bluish-purple on a silver band. At first, she thought it was glass and was careful "not to break it." The stone has remained wrapped around her finger ever since.

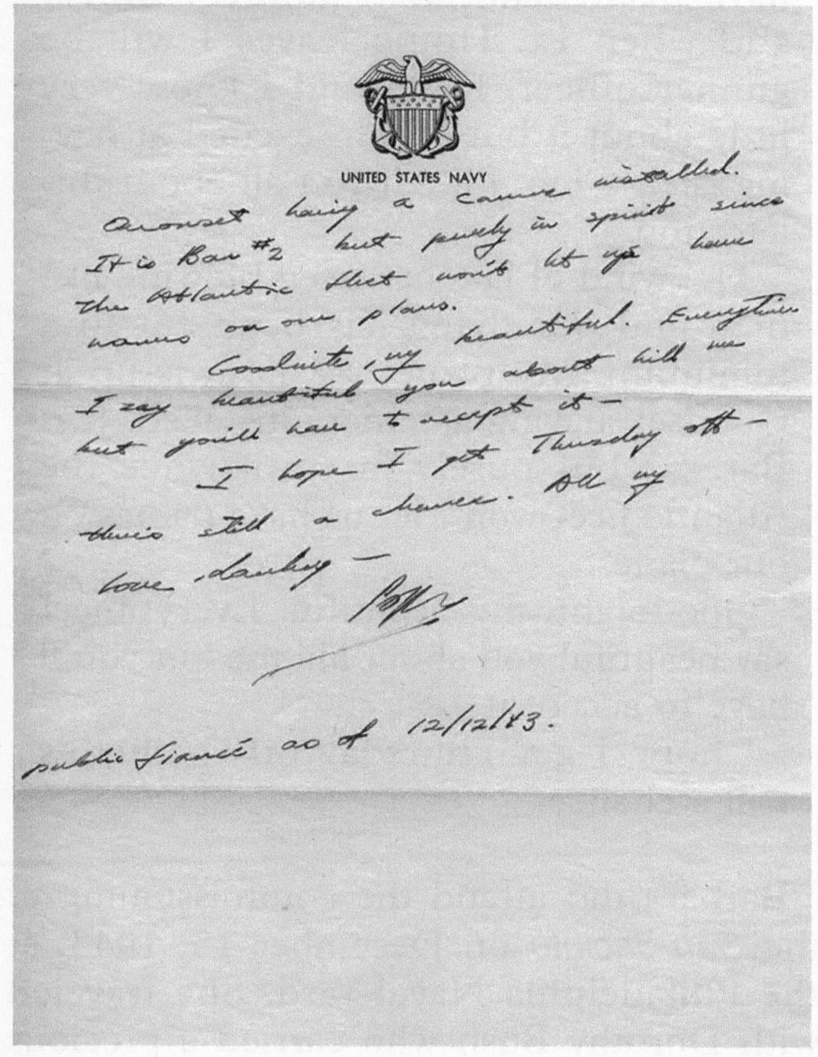

UNITED STATES NAVY

Quonset having a canoe installed.
It is Bar #2 but purely in spirit since
the Atlantic fleet won't let us have
canoes on our planes.

Goodnite, my beautiful. Everytime
I say beautiful you about kill me
but you'll have to accept it —

I hope I get Thursday off —
there's still a chance. All my
love, darling —

Poppy

public fiancé as of 12/12/43.

The Captain and Officers of the

U. S. S. San Jacinto

request the honour of the presence of

Miss Barbara Pierce

on the occasion of the commissioning of the

U. S. S. San Jacinto

December fifteenth, nineteen forty-three

at two forty-five P. M.

Philadelphia Navy Yard, Philadelphia, Pennsylvania

Guest of Ens. Bush.

Barbara's invitation to the commissioning of the San Jacinto.

Nine: Halfway Across the World

In the fall of 1943, Barbara started her first year at Smith College. She immersed easily and was chosen to lead the women's soccer team as captain. George liked to joke that she was the "Queen of Northampton." A few months into her school year, George hopped on the train from New York for a spontaneous visit. He arrived in Northampton at 9:00 p.m. and she had to be in by 10:15 p.m. "Barbara was at the station looking so cute in her . . . polo coat and sporty big shoes. We walked up to Tyler and I met the house mother and a couple of the girls. Barbara had to be in at 10:15. I slept at sort of a boarding house across the road from Tyler," wrote George.

After the December commissioning, the *San Jacinto* sailed to Norfolk, Virginia, where George's squadron, VT-51, continued to train. In March, they were granted a five-day leave, and George took off for where everyone he loved was — home. He knew this would be his last visit before deployment and he didn't take a minute for granted. "I hated to leave and only hope that the skipper's estimate for eight or nine months is nearer correct than the dreary twelve-month prediction that goes around. Barbara never looked more beautiful than when I had to leave her Tuesday nite. It was indeed not fun to have to look in those beautiful big eyes and say goodbye, not knowing when I would see her again," he wrote home on March 23, 1944.

In March 1944, the *San Jacinto* left the naval base and sailed toward the war. On board, VT-51 began training for night missions. In the middle of the ocean on a moonless night, the horizon disappeared and the sea and sky merged to pitch black. George was directed to land on the darkened carrier; it was exactly what he'd trained for. "It was impossible to see the water, so it was necessary to check and recheck your instruments," George wrote to his mother. Only two pilots did not succeed. "Ours is the first CVL outfit to qualify at night — quite a distinction. Our fighters qualified fifteen of their people Sunday nite so all in all the 'braid' seems fairly well pleased with air group 51. I hope this

Barbara at Smith.

doesn't mean we are going to operate extensively at nite."

"This is the last farewell I guess, Mum. I have a feeling that we may not be out too long — in fact I sort of think we may get back by Xmas. We have known that this time would eventually roll around. I have not actually dreaded it, but I sure have enjoyed . . . being able to get home every so often. God knows that I don't want to leave you all and my darling Barbara, but I would not change now if I could and I know that you really would not want me to stay behind. I have enough happiness stored up in me to last me easily [through] the time I will be gone."

George's increasing proximity to the war-front inspired moments of simple gratitude aboard the *San Jacinto.* During the day, when he wasn't working, George exercised on the top deck, or read one of the novels his mother had given to him before he left. On nights when there was no land in sight, George made his way outside to stare at the stars and he'd think of Barbara. "I have felt actually happy all evening — this balmy nite must have a contagious effect on me . . . Must be your son's in love, Ma," he wrote on April 2, 1944.

The *San Jacinto* approached the Panama Canal, where they stopped long enough for the crew to explore. George picked up few gifts for his family back home, including a watch for his younger brother Bucky and a purse for Barbara. Then the ship slid through to the Pacific Ocean, marking George's first time on that sea. "Well, how they got Pacific out of Pacific I don't know. So far the sea has been pretty rough," he wrote home on April 15, 1944.

On April 20, 1944, the *San Jacinto* reached Pearl Harbor, where the damage from the 1941 attack remained. "The ships were still in the water . . . everywhere the skeletons of ships as if to demand remembrance and warn us of our own mortality," remembered George. By May, the *San Jac* had reached its destination — Majuro Harbor in the Marshall Islands.

Before George had experienced combat, he flew over the secluded cluster of green and blue specks that compose the Marshall Islands and he thought they almost looked serene. "Seems terribly funny to fly around and see tiny islands — so peaceful looking and so insignificant looking — and then realize that they were stages for battles," he wrote home on May 12, 1944.

George had named his plane *Barbara* before, but only in spirit since the pilots weren't allowed to paint on the planes. However, out in the South Pacific the rules were different. "The pacific fleet apparently allows names on planes so mine is now 'Hamp Queen,' " he wrote home on May 5, 1944. A cute nod to his nickname for Barbara. For some reason, though, *Hamp Queen* was ditched and a few weeks later *Bar II* was painted in yellow letters. *Bar II* didn't last long. After being shot at and losing oil, George executed an emergency water landing. George and his crew were picked up by a destroyer and shuttled back to the *San Jacinto; Bar II* sunk into the South Pacific. On to *Barbara III.*

The missions were always dangerous, and one event shook the squadron when Jim Wykes and his crew were lost at sea (never to be found). He wrote his mom about his grief on May 26, 1944:

> Here is some distressing news, which I hate to report. Jim Wykes is now officially missing. It has affected those of us who knew him very deeply as he was a fellow whom everyone liked. I, personally, have far from given up hope and as I write this I can't help but feel that he will turn up. He may fall into enemy hands, but at least he'll still have his life. All we can do is

Plane over the Marshall Islands.

George, in the cockpit of Barbara III.

George's (back row, second from right) squadron — photo signed by the pilots.

hope. His family has been notified so it's O.K. to mention it now. He disappeared on a search mission — with him were 2 crewmen, both good men; one of whom had just become a father shortly before leaving the states. News like this is unpleasant, but I guess I'll just have to learn to take it. Jim was my closest friend on the ship — a fellow whom I was very fond of. There is a definite hope — perhaps he will even turn up soon. Well I must stop for now and get up on security watch, with much love to all the family, I am devotedly yours, Pop.

He longed to tell his parents and Barbara of where he was and what his missions entailed, but couldn't for obvious security reasons. In some cases, in George's letters, sentences, and words were cut or blacked out in places where he had revealed too much detail. Memories of home brought him great comfort, especially thinking about his beloved Kennebunkport and the previous magical summer. On June 10, 1944, he wrote:

> What are your plans for the summer, etc. I hope you get to K[ennebunk]port for a while anyway. Gosh I had a marvelous time there those two weeks last summer but then why shouldn't I have — with most of the family there, that 'salt air,' that food and oh yes having Bar there may have had something to do with it . . . As far as elapsed time making a difference in my feelings towards Bar I was sure when I left I'd never change, and now as each day passes I am even more sure. I love her so desperately that nothing could ever change my feelings — of that I'm convinced.

Back at Smith, Barbara couldn't concentrate. She tuned in to broadcasts, gathered as much news as possible — weeding out rumors or bad reports — and read between the lines of George's letters. She worried, even though there was nothing she could do. Daydreaming helped. Her mind drifted to wedding details and her future as Mrs. George H. W. Bush. Little else seemed to matter, especially her studies, and her grades suffered. Marvin Pierce called the freshman dean to explain his daughter's shortcomings but Barbara dropped out of Smith in the fall of 1944. She promised her parents that she would go back to school in January after the wedding. Her mother was especially adamant that she finish her schooling. She never did. It's a decision she later regretted, but at the time, she was too absorbed in her life with George.

The couple set a wedding date for December 17, 1944. George's time in the Pacific was no longer the adventure he had originally imagined; it was a job that he took seriously, but that he couldn't wait to complete. He had a life to get back to, and soon a wife — this anticipated future carried him through the long days at sea and his dangerous missions.

What he and Barbara didn't know is that

he wouldn't make it back home by December 17.

TEN: WORD FROM HOME

Barbara Bush kept everything. Her scrapbooks occupy an aisle in the George Bush Library and Museum in College Station, Texas — all 181 of them. Each is organized chronologically and is filled with photographs, letters, newspaper clippings, and cards. Stuffed into one envelope was a wishbone from their first turkey on Thanksgiving while they were at Yale, yet to be broken.

Unfortunately, after moving so many times around the country and even across the world, Barbara misplaced all but one of her letters from George during World War II and, of course, hers are gone as well. However, Dorothy Bush kept almost all of the letters George sent to Grove Lane, and those folded documents are now kept safely at the library in Texas.

During the war, letters carried a soldier through the darkest days.

The chirpy bugle call would signal that mail had arrived on the *San Jacinto,* and servicemen would be anxious for any word from home. Two or three letters at once was a fantastic day. Luckily, George had loyal pen-pals.

> "Joy of joys got a letter from Bar and one from Dad today — how nice it is to get mail,"
>
> — GEORGE, WRITING HOME ON APRIL 2, 1944

Letters were important for morale. To see the handwriting of loved ones and to hear their voices in letters comforted and reinforced soldiers' reasons for fighting. For George, he loved hearing from Barbara at school, and thinking of their wedding in the coming months brought him tremendous happiness. He also loved to hear about his little brother's baseball games, and even Phillips Academy and Yale games — he asked his mother to send him newspaper clippings of some of the games. Hearing about Kennebunkport in the summer or Greenwich in the spring, brought back many emotions for George and often reminded him what he was fighting to protect. Even scenes from less than a year before seemed like they existed in a sunny distant past. On June 1, 1944, he wrote: "Greenwich sounds beautiful at this time of year. I can picture everything so plainly: tennis, dinner on the porch, the summer evenings, etc."

In his bunk, George would cling to the pieces of paper that were once in the hands of Barbara and had traveled halfway across the world to reach him. He had a photograph of Barbara beside his bunk and his mother had sent a few new ones of the family when he was in the South Pacific. He had a few other pictures tucked into his wallet. "I find myself hauling them out for a good stare," he confessed in a letter home on April 15, 1944.

The *San Jacinto* would be out at sea for long stretches, and for George it would feel like forever since he had heard from home, but there were few greater feelings than arriving at port and having a stack waiting for you, as George wrote to his mother:

> "Being out at sea is always exciting and fortunately the time goes by quite quickly, but it's always a pleasure to hit port and

get some news from home. I loved hearing about the ball game . . . also about seeing Bar. I am so glad she dropped by to see you all. I am awfully lucky I appreciate that fact no end, but sometimes I miss Bar so terribly much that I begin to wonder (not seriously) . . . I have been doing quite a bit of reading whenever the opportunity permits which isn't very often except in port. Also plenty of thinking about the future, etc. Right now all I really would care to do would be to be married to Bar and be near home doing anything at all."

Understanding the importance of consistent news from home, in the summer of 1942, the United States launched V-Mail, a system modeled on the British Airgraph Service. Americans at home and deployed military personnel wrote letters on one-sided stationery. Those letters were forwarded to the closest processing centers, where they were photographed on to 16 millimeter film. The reels of film were then delivered to the receiving stations overseas; one reel contained over a thousand letters, which made cargo much lighter than traditional letters and delivery quicker because the film could be carried on airplanes. At the stations, V-Mail letters were printed and finally dispatched to homes in the United States and to American military service members in Europe and in the Pacific. According to the Smithsonian's National Postal Museum, over the course of World War II, over a billion V-Mails were delivered.

Despite the improved system's efficiency, especially in times of combat, deliveries could be slow moving. Sometimes George and Barbara would go weeks without hearing anything, and other times, they would receive a stack. Everything George sent to Barbara was also censored. Any information that might be useful to the enemy would be blacked out. Most men knew not to enclose such information. Also, many did not want to report the entire truth of what they had seen during the war, so as not to upset their loved ones.

The most difficult letters were the ones that took the longest to arrive. The hardest stretch was in September 1944. Barbara had not heard from George for weeks. Then she received a letter from Doug West of George's squadron. George had been shot down off the island of Chichi Jima, he wrote. Doug spotted George swimming to his life raft and a submarine had been alerted of his coordinates. Barbara called Dorothy — "We were frantic." The next three days seemed to last a lifetime.

On September 2, 1944, George's squadron left the *San Jacinto* at 7:15 a.m. on a mission to take out a communications tower on Chichi Jima. A large explosion came from below and shook the plane. "The plane was lifted forward and we were enveloped in flames," George told author Joe Hyams. They had been hit. Before turning away from the target, George finished the mission, unloading four 500-pound bombs. "Hit the silk," he yelled on the intercom, telling his two crewmen, John Delaney and Ted White, to bail. Once he felt like he had given them time to jump, George abandoned the Avenger 2,000 feet above the water, but the wind carried him towards the back of the plane and his head and his parachute collided with the tail. With a gash to his forehead and a punctured chute he descended quickly toward the water. When George hit the surface, Lieutenant Commander D. J. Melvin dipped down toward the water in his plane to point out the location of the raft. George swam to it and climbed aboard. His squadron held back an enemy boat that was racing out to pick him up, and George paddled as hard as he could.

"I had some dye marker attached to my life jacket and also there was some in the raft so I sprinkled a bit of that on the water so the planes could see me easily. I took inventory of my supplies and discovered that I had no water. The water had broken open when the raft fell from the plane I imagine. I had a mirror, some other equipment, and also was wearing my own gun and knife."

— GEORGE BUSH

An hour passed. Still no sign of Delaney or White, and no ships on the horizon. His squadron's planes were no longer searching, which indicated to George that they probably didn't make it out of the bomber. "I'm afraid I was pretty much of a sissy

A Grumman "Avenger" Navy torpedo bomber.

about it cause I sat in my raft and sobbed for a while. It bothers me so very much," he wrote the very next day on September 3, 1944. "I did tell them and when I bailed out I felt that they must have gone, and yet now I feel so terribly responsible for their fate. . . . Perhaps as the days go by it will all change and I will be able to look upon it in a different light."

Another hour passed and "what appeared to be a small black dot, only a hundred yards away" emerged. *Was he imagining things?* "The dot grew larger. First a periscope, then the conning tower, then the hull of a submarine emerged from the depths," remembered George.

It was the U.S.S. *Finback.* Dazed, Bush was pulled aboard by five crew members. "Let's get below. The skipper wants to get the hell out of here," said a crewman. The entire rescue was captured by Ensign Bill Edwards, photographic officer, who later created an eight-millimeter film of the event.

On board the *Finback,* George wrote letters daily, trying to sort out what had happened. At night, he tossed and turned — *did he do the right thing?* Everything happened so quickly, it was hard to make sense of it all. "Last night I rolled and tossed. I kept reliving the whole experience. My

George's rescue by the U.S.S. Finback.

heart aches for the families of those two boys with me," he wrote Dorothy and Prescott on September 3, 1944.

By September 5, he was assigned to two

deck watches. George wrote his parents that when they were submerged he was "utterly useless," but up top on the tower he could "sweep the sea and skies pretty well" with a pair of binoculars. Late in the evening until just before dawn, shielded by darkness, the *Finback* would come up and float on the ocean's surface. George enjoyed the midnight to 4 a.m. shift. The stillness offered him space to collect his thoughts. "The sub moved like a porpoise, water lapping over its bow, the sea changing colors, first jet black, then sparkling white," he recalled.

"It reminded me of home and our family vacations in Maine. The nights were clear

and the stars so bright you felt you could touch them. It was hypnotic. There was peace, calm, beauty — God's therapy."
— GEORGE BUSH

The memories of John Delaney and Ted White, who did not survive the mission and therefore never made it home to loved ones, have remained with George his entire life. Back on the *San Jacinto,* no one mentioned the mission to George; everyone knew the unbearable tragedies of war and they never wanted to add to his guilt. However, George never stopped remembering them; decades later while he was president, he invited their families to visit the White House.

"I still don't understand the 'logic' of war — why some survive and others are lost in their prime. But that month on the *Finback* gave me time to reflect, to go deep inside myself and search for answers. As you grow older and try to retrace the steps that made you the person you are, the signposts to look for are those special times of insight, even awakening. I remember my days and nights aboard the U.S.S *Finback* as one of those times — maybe the most important of them all."

— GEORGE BUSH

UNITED STATES PACIFIC FLEET
Commander Second Carrier Task Force,
PACIFIC FLEET

* * *

In the name of the President of the United States, the Commander, Second Carrier Task Force, United States Pacific Fleet, presents the DISTINGUISHED FLYING CROSS to

LIEUTENANT (JUNIOR GRADE) GEORGE HERBERT WALKER BUSH
UNITED STATES NAVAL RESERVE

FOR SERVICE AS SET FORTH IN THE FOLLOWING

CITATION

"For distinguishing himself by heroism and extraordinary achievement while participating in aerial flights in line of his profession as pilot of a torpedo plane during the attacks by United States Naval Forces against Japanese installations in the vicinity of the Bonin Islands on 2 September 1944. He led one section of a four plane division which attacked a radio station. Opposed by intense anti-aircraft fire his plane was hit and set afire as he commenced his dive. In spite of smoke and flames from the fire in his plane, he continued in his dive and scored damaging bomb hits on the radio station, before bailing out of his plane. His courage and complete disregard for his own safety, both in pressing home his attack in the face of intanse and accurate anti-aircraft fire, and in continuing in his dive on the target after being hit and his plane on fire, were at all times in keeping with the highest traditions of the United States Naval Service."

J. S. McCain
Vice Admiral, U. S. Navy

George's citation for the Distinguished Flying Cross signed by Senator John McCain's father, John S. McCain.

When I'm visiting my childhood home in Bethesda, Maryland, I like to wander downstairs to the basement and over to the closets near the garage. This is where my mom keeps scrapbooks and memories from over the years. I find the box labeled "Letters from Ganny and Gampy" and start reading.

In this day and age, with technology at the forefront, oftentimes the art of letter writing is forgotten. My grandparents have kept it alive, at least in their lives. Their grandchildren and children have all been recipients of special letters over the years. They come for different reasons: welcome to the world, I'm thinking of you, Hi — how are you?, Here's a small gift — don't tell your siblings.

Here is special letter that Gampy wrote to my mom and dad, five days before I was born, when he was vice president. A perfect example of my sweet grandfather.

November 14, 1986

Dear Doro and Billy,

Maybe, just maybe, by the time you get this letter there will be new joy in this world. Mum is coming your way, and I wish I were there. I know it looks different, my heading off to Notre Dame as it takes on Penn State; but I mean it. For you see the only thing that really matters for me is the breath of our new loved one.

In a selfish sense I'm glad I'm not there for the play by play — "O.K. Bill breathe in, blow out, breathe in, hang in there"; or great, Doro a couple of more centimeters of dilation, oh my soul, and the baby will be on its way. No, I'm not good at the mechanics. But I'd love to see the first eye open, hear the first cry — and see you two as you see George for the first time or is it Georgette? All I know is the kid is coming on in to a life of great love — oh maybe Sam will have to level a rock or two at her/his head to give the kid a little leadership; but I'm talking all encompassing love — the kind that makes you want to run and jump into your Dad's arms when you're hurt, or wants you to whisper to Mom, after you've been bad, I love you.

When I hear Sam say hi Ba Ba, Iran seems inconsequential, the White House is blurred, the future seems not to matter; and so it will be tomorrow or the next day when we have [someone else] to love, to laugh with, to wonder at . . . [say Fred] do you [know] what my last [grandkid] did — the little weiner pulled my glasses off and looked into my eyes and smiled — no kidding I know the kid loves me.

This is life its ownself. This is our very heartbeat, this is what matters most . . . so good luck my little tuna, oops my little peppers, good luck Bill, you have given us great happiness in our lives — great true all encompassing happiness. Some day, when all my politics are over, I will try hard, and so will Bar to give you back a little joy. Maybe we can do some sitting, maybe we can wipe away a tear or two when the twins pick on my Sam and my ________.

But whatever we will love them as we do you, and in so doing we will know a true happiness that many are denied.

Devotedly,
Dad

ELEVEN: A TIME FOR CELEBRATION

George returned to the *San Jacinto* on November 2, 1944 — eight weeks after being shot down. He could have returned home, but he was anxious to get back to his squadron and his mission. When he climbed aboard, he received a warm welcome first from the skipper and everyone followed behind. He would soon learn that another life had been lost, Tom Waters, who was killed in action.

Men came to find him to welcome him back. He considered the greeting to be "one of the happiest moments of my life — I really mean that," he wrote home on November 3, 1944. One pleasant discovery upon his return was that his mail had piled up in his absence. "All during the time I was talking to the boys I kept eagerly eyeing my sky-high stack of mail. I was anxious to pounce upon it to find out how everyone is. The mail lived up to the highest expectations — I sorted them all and read [through] them — I still haven't read them over, something I definitely want to do," he wrote home. While he was aboard the *Finback* and then later in R&R, he had been longing for a letter from Barbara; he had not heard from her for months. Once he was alone on his bunk, he tore through the envelopes from Barbara and his family, eager to to read the stories from home within.

In December, good news reached VT-51. After George's 58 combat missions, his squadron was given orders to return home. He called Barbara from Hawaii to tell her he was on his way; they could finally get married.

While December 17 had come and gone, Barbara didn't seem to miss a beat back at home. She was no longer at Smith and dedicated the fall to making wedding arrangements. She received word from George that they could set a date, and in neat cursive on each invitation she wrote in: "Saturday, the sixth of January."

Before walking his daughter down the aisle, Marvin organized a special lunch with her in New York City. Even though they were only a few train stops away, Barbara "rarely went into the city" and even more

Mr. and Mrs. Marvin Pierce
request the honour of your presence
at the marriage of their daughter
Barbara
to
George Herbert Walker Bush
Lieutenant, junior grade, United States Naval Reserve
Saturday, the sixth of January
at four o'clock
The Presbyterian Church
and afterwards at the reception
The Apawamis Club
Rye, New York

R.S.V.P.

George and Barbara's wedding invitation.

rare was an afternoon alone with her father, but he had wanted to leave his third child with the wisdom he had acquired after four children and many married years. "He talked to me about marriage and the commitment it meant," she wrote. He also gave her sound advice on marital finances and how to avoid the stresses of such materialism and maintain what is truly important — love.

Another pearl he lent her that day was about rearing a close-knit family: "He also told me that the three most important things you can give your children are: the best education, a good example, and all the love in the world. He certainly lived by that rule and gave us all that and more, including trust," she recalled.

After eight months of separation, Barbara received the phone call that made her heart race. It was George; he had landed in New

George and Barbara reunited at last at Christmas.

Barbara with parents.

York City and he was on his way to Rye, New York. She rushed to the station.

"No reunion could have been scripted more perfectly," remembered George. "I arrived Christmas Eve. There were tears, laughs, hugs, joy, the love and warmth of family in a holiday setting."

The day George and Barbara had mutually dreamed of — separated by an ocean and a war — had finally arrived. On Saturday, January 6, 1945, at 4 p.m., with her arm through Marvin's, Barbara walked down the aisle of the First Presbyterian Church in Rye, New York, to George. She was in an

Bush family photo at wedding.

ivory satin gown and George was in his navy uniform as they exchanged promises in front of family and friends. The reception was held at the Apawamis Club a little over a mile away. Chandeliers lit the room and dark green ivy was festively draped from the arched doorways as George and Barbara danced in the same room they had danced three years before, this time as husband and wife.

The weight of the times was not altogether absent even on such a happy occasion. In long green dresses, the many bridesmaids outnumbered George's ushers. Men who were on the list were not able to attend, including Barbara's brother, Jimmy, who was unable to get leave.

After the wedding, the Bushes took a train to the Cloister, a resort on Sea Island on Georgia's coast. Both the wedding and honeymoon were organized around and came to a close because of the war and after a brief, sunny hiatus, George had to report for duty. This time, however, Mrs. Barbara Bush was going with him.

Barbara and George cutting the cake.

Barbara and George on their honeymooon.

"I am so very lucky having my 'bieber' here with me. In spite of being a worrier over things, even if we had no roof over our heads, I would still be happiest having Bar here. I shall not burden her with my worrying, Mum. I assure you."
— GEORGE, IN A LETTER TO HIS MOTHER

George and Barbara set up temporary homes from Michigan to Maine as his new squadron, VT 153, formed. On May 8, 1945, V-E Day had triggered celebrations, but the battles in the Pacific continued and George trained for an invasion of Japan.

As summer set in, George was sent to Norfolk, Virginia. Barbara met him there and they rented a basement apartment that came with a shared bath. Living arrangements were hard to come by for couples in the service because they were very much in demand. Nonetheless, this particular location suited them — right across the street was the Princess Anne Country Club and for six dollars a month, they were members.

In each short stint, the young couple experienced the intimacies of married life: shared meals, lazy Saturdays reading side by side, and evenings double-dating with friends. This was what George had pictured while aboard the *San Jacinto.* Everything was falling into place, and it was nearly impossible to imagine George leaving for the South Pacific again.

On August 6 and 9, 1945, President Harry Truman made the decision to drop two atomic bombs on Hiroshima and Nagasaki. The Japanese surrendered on August 15, 1945.

At 7 p.m. the announcement of Japan's surrender reached Virginia Beach. Almost immediately uniformed soldiers flooded the streets. Loved ones — even strangers — embraced, and danced around cars. Everything paused for the celebrations. George and Barbara joined in the spectacle, and then later that evening filed into a local church to pray for those who had lost their lives and were not there to witness the joy of the finale.

COMMANDER AIR FORCE
ATLANTIC FLEET

ADMINISTRATIVE OFFICE
U. S. NAVAL AIR STATION
NORFOLK, VIRGINIA
3 October 1945

20 September 1945

Dear Mr. Bush:

I am cognizant of the able manner in which you performed your duties while attached to Torpedo Squadron ONE HUNDRED FIFTY THREE from February 1945 to August 1945. The results achieved in your work evidenced initiative, sound judgment, and devotion to duty, and your fine spirit of cooperation contributed to the smooth working of that organization. You have made a substantial contribution to the successful operations of Air Force, Atlantic Fleet, and it is a pleasure to express my esteem for your faithful and efficient performance of duty.

Appropriate orders have been issued releasing you from active duty. Your return to civil life affords me this opportunity to thank you for the valuable services you have rendered to your country. To you, and to all like you, who answered to the call of duty in time of need, who subordinated personal desires to the winning of the war, and who served faithfully and effectively, your country will always be grateful.

Very sincerely,

P. N. L. BELLINGER,
Vice Admiral, U. S. Navy.

Lieutenant (jg) George H. W. BUSH, USNR
Torpedo Squadron ONE HUNDRED FIFTY THREE
C/o Fleet Post Office
New York, New York

Letter releasing George from active duty.

Four years of warfare had come to an end, and life for the Bushes was just beginning.

Twelve: Then There Were Three

George had been admitted to Yale when he was enrolled at Phillips Academy, but he decided to defer his acceptance and join the navy. When the war ended, Yale readmitted all 1,500 men who had deferred as well as 900 who left for the war as freshman; by the following year the school would nearly double the size of its student body. The G.I. Bill paid George's tuition and Yale Studies for Returning Service Men, a program established by the university faculty, allowed him and other veterans to graduate in seven terms.

George was following the academic path of his father, Prescott, great-grandfather, James Smith Bush, and a few uncles who attended the prestigious institution in New Haven, Connecticut, but his wasn't the typical college experience. George was twenty-one years old, he had a wife, and by the summer, a son, George Walker Bush, who

While at Yale, George and Barbara welcomed George Walker Bush to the family.

was born on July 6, 1946. The war had demanded separation and patience, now they were together at last, and when it came to Yale, they focused on getting in and out and on with their life. Since the student body ranged in age and life experience, the faculty went out of their way to bring similar groups together. George and Barbara were invited to a dinner for married couples on campus, and they lived in an old converted mansion on Hillhouse Avenue with twelve other families with young children.

As George worked toward his degree in economics, he and Barbara got involved on campus. His senior year, he was tapped for Skull and Bones, a secret society on campus known for selecting budding leaders. Barbara worked at the campus bookstore and also audited a course by John Marshall Phillips on American architecture, furniture,

Dinner party with friends.

and art. While they were anxious to exit student life, it wasn't all work and no play. They had a number of dinner parties, and in the fall of that first year, they hosted their first Thanksgiving. "I do not remember many of the details, but I know we had a turkey and we did not have a dining room," recalled Barbara. Guests found a place wherever — couches, chairs, the floors, and Barbara utilized every pan, dish, and piece of silverware. The stack of dirty dishes overwhelmed the sink of their shared kitchen. The informal, unfussy gathering would be the first of many.

On campus, George and Barbara were young, married, and popular, which is why they were the perfect candidates for a modeling gig. In the summer of 1948, George and Barbara Bush appeared in several advertisements for Bates Fabrics, Inc., which was based in Lewiston, Maine. The company had just released a new line of comforters and matching drapes targeted at college students. The series of advertisements ran in August and September in *Life, Harper's Bazaar, Calling All Girls, Vogue, Mademoiselle, McCall's, Parents, Seventeen,* and *Good Housekeeping.* It was their first step into the spotlight.

George also played first base for the Yale Bulldogs and his senior year he was voted team captain. The 1947 and 1948 Yale teams were competitive; they made it to the national championships but lost to California the first year and Southern Cal the second. When Barbara was younger her mother would loyally follow the Dodgers. At the end of the night, "she'd sniff your breath and tell you the score of the Dodgers game," remembered Scott Pierce. The love of the game brushed off on Barbara; she at-

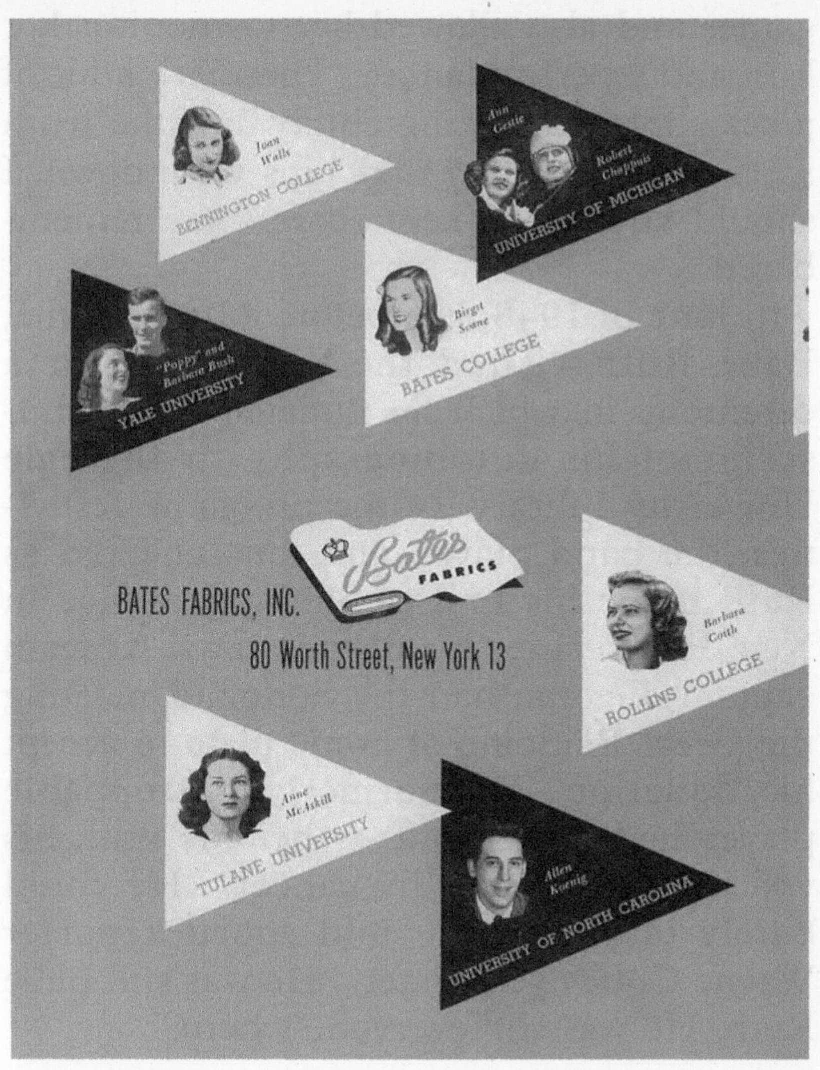

One of the ads for Bates Fabrics featuring George and Barbara.

tended all of George's home games. Armed with a pencil and paper, she watched intently while keeping score. The detailed art kept her involved during a number of long games and also allowed her to monitor her husband's performance. "There are a lot of jokes about his hitting ability, but the truth is, George hit when the chips were down. I should know — I kept score," she remembered.

In June of 1948, just before a home game, Babe Ruth visited the Yale Field for a ceremony in which he donated the manuscript of his autobiography to the Yale University Library. In the pre-game festivities, the band played and fans cheered as Ruth made his first public appearance in New Haven since his playing days. As team captain, George had the honor of meeting the Great Bambino at home plate to accept his donation. The formerly unstoppable player had grown old — he was frail, his voice compromised by cancer. "He could barely talk," George told sports reporter Wayne Coffey years later. "He was still Babe Ruth. He was still everyone's hero."

When George was in the Oval Office, he kept his Yale baseball glove in his desk drawer. The love of the game rubbed off on George W., too, who went on to own the Texas Rangers. As is traditional for presidents since the beginning of the twentieth century, George also threw out a number of

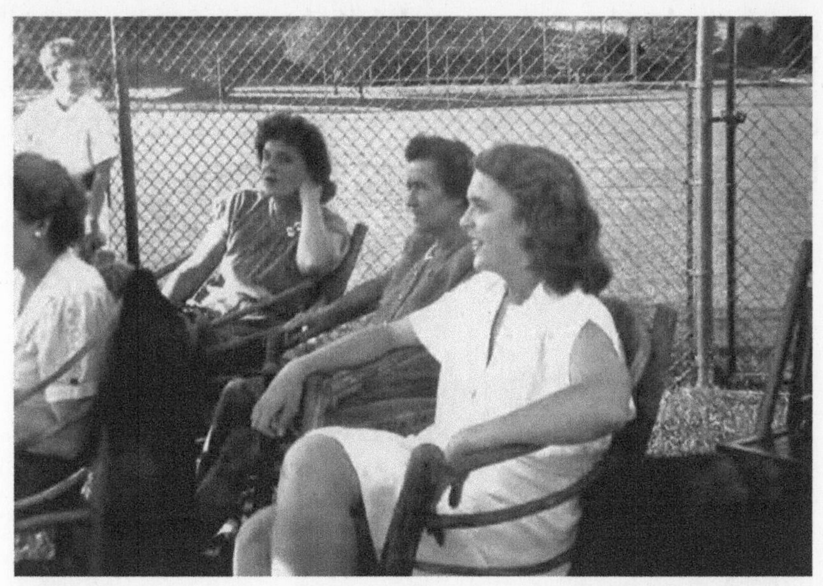

Barbara watching one of George's baseball games.

first pitches in professional games. In 1989, on opening day at Memorial Stadium in Baltimore, the president hurried across the field as his tie flapped in the wind; he threw what the *New York Times* called "a little high and outside" pitch to catcher Mickey Tettleton.

Decades later in 2015, George and Barbara were honored at the third game of the World Series in Houston. Fans cheered as the forty-first president and first lady made their way to home plate for the first pitch. Time had again revealed the age of two leaders: George was in a neck brace and confined to a wheelchair, vascular parkinsonism had conquered his leg muscles, and Barbara maneuvered slowly across the dirt and grass with her walker as the crowd brightened with applause. After the pitch,

George with Babe Ruth.

George grabbed Barbara's hand and they waved.

> "Breaking away meant just that — living on our own. I'd saved up three thousand dollars in the Navy. Not much, but enough to get us started independently. We were young, still in our early twenties, and we wanted to make our own way, our own mistakes, and shape our own future."
>
> — GEORGE BUSH

In the spring of George's last year at Yale, the couple dreamed about the future. There was the version they knew: Building a life in the suburbs of New York, a job in the city a train ride away, friends and family a few miles down the road. He even had a few job offers, so the idea was within reach. However, the Bushes were intrigued by the scripts that were less familiar. There was the romantic thought of owning a farm. They had both read Louis Bromfield's *The Farm* and had visions of an old farmhouse, working with their own hands outside, and living off the land, but once they did the numbers and realized the sum of a large upfront investment, the countryside venture didn't seem to make sense. "No matter how we looked at it, though, George and Barbara Farms came off as a high-risk, no-yield investment," recalled George.

Barbara during their Yale days.

Around the time that they were imagining the possibilities, George received a letter from his childhood friend, Gerry Bemiss, who had heard that George was considering becoming a priest. That was not on the long list of possibilities, but George wrote to his friend while he sorted out his plan.

Dear Gerry,

We have a while this afternoon before train time so I shall respond to your interesting letter. I can't imagine where you ever heard that I was going into the ministry. I have never even thought about the cloth — only a tablecloth or loincloth. Seriously I would be curious to know where you heard about it.

Right now I am bewildered to say the least. My mind is in a turmoil. I want to do something of value and yet I have to and want to make money — after George goes through 3 squares every day, one's wallet becomes thin and worn. I have thought of teaching, but right now it seems to me that it would be confining and not challenging enough. Besides teaching would require further study almost immediately, and I am not prepared to study textbooks right now — perhaps later but not now.

So where does that leave me — no cloth, no books, perhaps a briefcase, I could work for Herby Walker in St. Louis — G.H. Walker & Co. investments etc. Some are fascinated, and genuinely so, by such a business. Perhaps I would be. Right now I do not know. It's not a basic business and yet it is important as long as we are living under a relatively free economic system. I am uncertain — I want to know and understand people, but the people I'd be doing business with in the investment business, I know to some degree now. I am not sure I wanted to capitalize completely on the benefits I received at birth — that is on the benefits of my social position. Such qualities as industriousness, integrity, etc. which I have or at least hope I have had inculcated into me by my parents, at least to some degree, (I hope) I do want to use, but doing well merely because I have had the opportunity to attend the same debut parties as some of my customers, does not appeal to me.

This may sound frightfully confused. Don't get me wrong. I am not preaching redistribution of wealth etc.; rather I am saying that I would hate to get caught in what could be a social and somewhat unproductive eddy. Perhaps I shall go with Walkers. If I go I shall work hard and long. Financially it would be fine — good starting pay, and fairly nice sledding ahead; but once again I just don't know.

Lastly I have this chance to go with Neil Mallon's Dresser Industries — perhaps to Texas. They make equipment for the oil and gas industries. They are basic. Texas would be new and exciting for a while — hard on Bar perhaps — and heaven knows many girls would bitch like blazes about such a proposed move — Bar's different though, Gerry. She lives quite frankly for Georgie and myself. She is wholly unselfish, beautifully tolerant of my weaknesses and idiosyncrasies, and ready to faithfully follow any course I [choose] . . . I haven't had a chance to make many shrewd moves in my young life, but when I married Bar I hit the proverbial jackpot. Her devotion overcomes me and I must often stop in my mad whirl around college etc. to see if I am considering her at all . . .

Anyway — the Dresser job at the moment has great appeal. I would be seeing new people, learning something of basic importance. What stands in the way of my flying headlong into it, is first — (I have to see Neil this month in Cleveland about pay and other not so minor details) and secondly the old question of is business what I want?

Well from all the above you can see that I don't know what I am going to do. Graduation is on Monday — then we go to Kalamazoo Michigan for the college world series in baseball. Down here at W. Salem we have just won the Eastern Championship . . . We were thrilled to win — It was all night baseball quite a change from day, but we played our best ball of the year and came through . . .

Your clerical maybe
but not clergical
friend —
Pop

After graduating in June 1948, George and Barbara decided on that third and final prospect: The one that excited them the most and even scared them a little — Texas.

Thirteen: Promises of West Texas

George and Barbara Bush have moved twenty-seven times and lived in eight houses in Texas alone. In her early nineties, when asked which was her favorite house, Barbara points to the floorboards of their current abode in the Tanglewood neighborhood of Houston, across the street from their son, Neil. Sunlight pokes through the trees and shines into their living room. On the floor is a needlepoint rug that took Barbara nine years to complete. Throughout the scene, she's hidden the initials of all of her grandchildren. Colorful Keds sneakers are in a pile by the door. The whole house is filled with family photographs and irreplaceable objects collected over a lifetime.

They moved to Texas in their early twenties, linking up with a new wave of young entrepreneurs who also had youthful families in tow. As the new families grew, so did the community and the Bushes took an active role — joining clubs, attending meetings, and teaching the next generation. They invested a lot of time and energy into the promise of West Texas.

Somewhere along the way, through all the moves, they placed less importance on their physical address. Texas had become home.

The Bushes' first Texas home was a two-room apartment with a shared bath on East Seventh Street in Odessa. In 1948, Odessa was small, flat, and surrounded by short-grass prairie. Drive out of town and the empty landscape stretched for miles, interrupted occasionally with towering derricks. Ten thousand feet below the surface was what every newcomer to Texas was after — oil.

"This West Texas is a fabulous place, Gerry. Fortunes can be made in the land end of the oil business, and of course can be lost."
— GEORGE BUSH WRITING TO A FRIEND

In 1901, the first geyser of black gold shot out of the Texas earth four miles south of Beaumont. The well produced seventeen

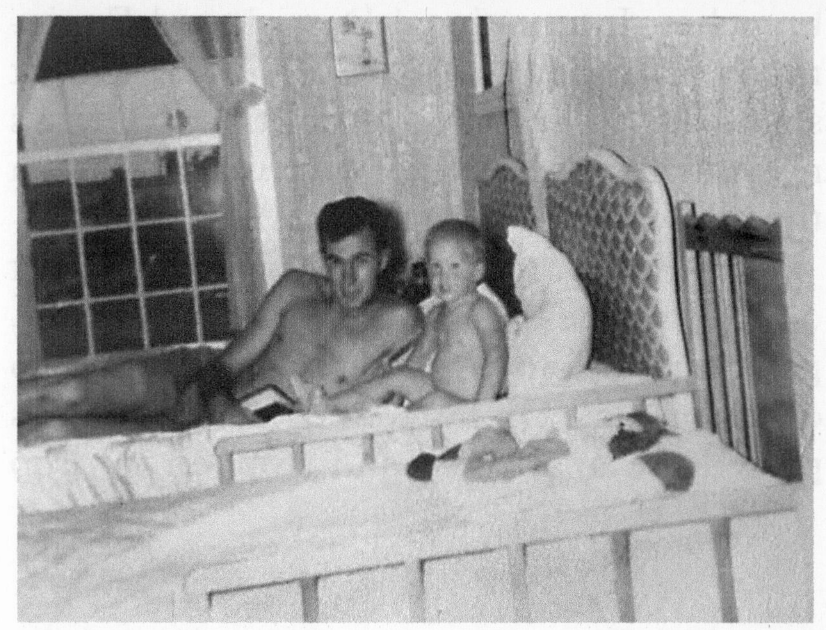

George and George W. in their small Texas apartment.

million barrels that first year and declared the southern state the epicenter of the oil boom. In the 1920s, the Permian Basin revealed more buried deposits and suddenly businessmen became very interested in the dusty towns of Midland and Odessa.

In the late forties, the Bushes were among the optimistic arrivals. Months earlier, family friend Neil Mallon had told George, West Texas was "the place for ambitious young people." Neil was the head of Dresser Industries, and he offered George a job as an equipment clerk at one of Dresser's branches, International Derrick and Equipment Company (IDECO). Neil didn't sugarcoat the entry-level position: "There's not much salary, but if you want to learn the oil business, it's a start."

As a trainee, George learned every aspect of the business — that meant sweeping, painting equipment, and driving around to check on rigs. On his rounds, he sometimes passed the apartment and stopped to drop

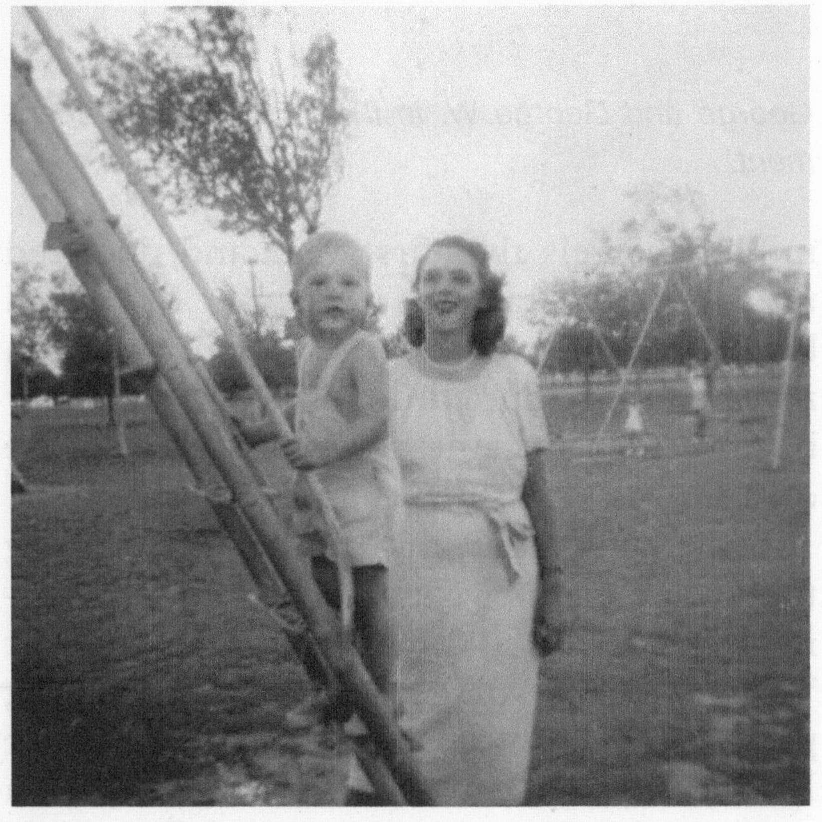

Barbara and George W. at the local park.

off flowers for Barbara. She wrote to her parents: "Pop has stopped twice on the road back from a rig — once to bring me some 'blackeyed susans' which revived beautifully and last about four days and today to bring me a weed that grows with no visible water. It has a dry root and dry stems — almost brittle. But it is covered with pretty white blossoms."

Even with frequent, happy letters home, Pauline believed her daughter was living in the middle of nowhere. She sent soap, cold cream, and other household items south. "As far as my mother was concerned, we could have been living in Russia," remembered Barbara.

In the tiny town, Barbara was beginning to make friends with neighbors. She was invited to afternoon bridge games as well as weekly church circles with some of the local wives. George W. was growing and constantly testing his parents. Barbara wrote home: "[He] sticks things into you, pinches, etc. and seems to thoroughly enjoy hurting us." When he was being naughty, George and Barbara decided an appropriate punishment was sending him to his room and shutting the door. One time, after the door was closed, George W. was being a little too quiet: "I went in to let him out — he had vanished — not magic, but just through the bathroom — into the [Casselman's] apt. and out their front door. He'd been out for about 15 min. and had completely forgotten the whole affair."

Of course, they loved him very much and all of their letters begin and end with stories of his funny sayings and new discoveries. "He is so wonderful, Mum," George wrote to his mother on October 20, 1948. "So cute and bright. Oh he has his mischievous and naughty spells, but I just can't picture what we would do without him."

There wasn't much to do, but Barbara kept busy with George W. She visited the library and checked out a number of books. She also tried her hand at household duties. Barbara wrote home:

> "I don't like to brag, but I am becoming a better housewife — our little house is really quite clean — and I get compliments on Georgie all the time . . . Pop's shirts and pants look pretty good — they aren't hard to do at all and we love our life. How I dreaded doing the washing and ironing at first. I did everything else and finally the clothes got washed — then did everything else all over again. Finally G.W.B. got sick about 3 weeks ago and Pop persuaded

me to have the ironing done (wasn't hard to do). With a clean stack I found that doing the washing and ironing twice a week in the mornings made it very easy. I have still not solved the starch problem. Twice I have used it and Pop's and G.W.B.'s clothes stood up by themselves."

On the weekends, they read *Time, Life, The Wall Street Journal,* and the local *Odessa American* — passing each other must-read pieces and later trading their opinions. Barbara told her parents about a new interest in "America's Town Meeting of the Air." After naptime, they walked to the park where two-year-old George W. loved the swings, slide, and merry-go-round. After sundown, cars would assemble at the local drive-in. Sunday mornings the family would get dressed up for church. Occasionally, George mingled with his IDECO colleagues and joined in on dove-hunting trips. "I think the men like him," Barbara informed her parents in a letter. "When I pick him up at work they always nod or wave to him. He seems to have the common touch — he is loved by all — especially me."

While George and Barbara were absorbed in George W., they longed to bring another baby into their Texas life that year. There

Barbara, George W., George, Dorothy, and Prescott in Texas.

was a glimmer of hope, but then Barbara suffered a miscarriage. On the most difficult days, they felt very far from home. George wrote to his mother in Connecticut on October 20, 1948:

"Bar is still not quite up to par. She gets little rest now with Georgie sick, but she is feeling better, and I think the worst of her troubles are over. I think that physically the last few days have been rough on her, and I know that her disappointment over this miscarriage was large. As I told you before we both are sort of hoping that we will have another child before too long. Bar thinks about it a lot, and foolishly worries too much. I don't like to have her upset. She is something, Mum, the way she never ever complains or even suggests that she would prefer to be elsewhere. She is happy, I know, but anyone would like to be around her own friends, be able to take at least a passing interest in clothes, parties, etc. She gets absolutely none of this. It is different for me, I have my job all day long with new things happening, but she is here in this small apt. with people whose interests cannot be at all similar to Bar's because they have never had any similar experiences. I continue to be amazed at her unselfishness, her ability to get along with absolutely anyone, and her wonderful way with Georgie. She never becomes cross or irritable at him, and never complains in any way about anything that we don't have, don't get to enjoy right now. It is one thing for her to be far from her home and friends, but it is still another greater thing to be able to live happily with people from such different backgrounds. I am so very lucky, Mum; I am grateful and I must always work to make Bar happy. She has made my life full and complete; she has given so much and never asked a return. How lucky I am!"

In 1949, at the request of Dresser, the family moved to California, where George learned to be a salesman at Pacific Pumps, another branch of the larger company. This position demanded a lot of driving and he got to know the California terrain. "I'd load up my car with bits and head one hundred miles up to Carrizo Plains or the Cuyama Valley, going from rig to rig, finding out what size bit the customer would need and what type of rock formation he'd be drilling into. I drove at least a thousand miles every week," he remembered.

One day, while George was at work, he had an urgent message from New York. It was Barbara's family: Marvin and Pauline Pierce had been in a car accident. Marvin was in the hospital, but Pauline was killed instantly. George raced home to break the news to Barbara. She tried to grapple with the fact that her mom was gone. "Sudden death is a terrible shock — but then all death is a struggle and a shock," she wrote.

Barbara was at last pregnant with their second child. When Marvin recovered, he and the rest of the family decided she should not make the trip back East for the

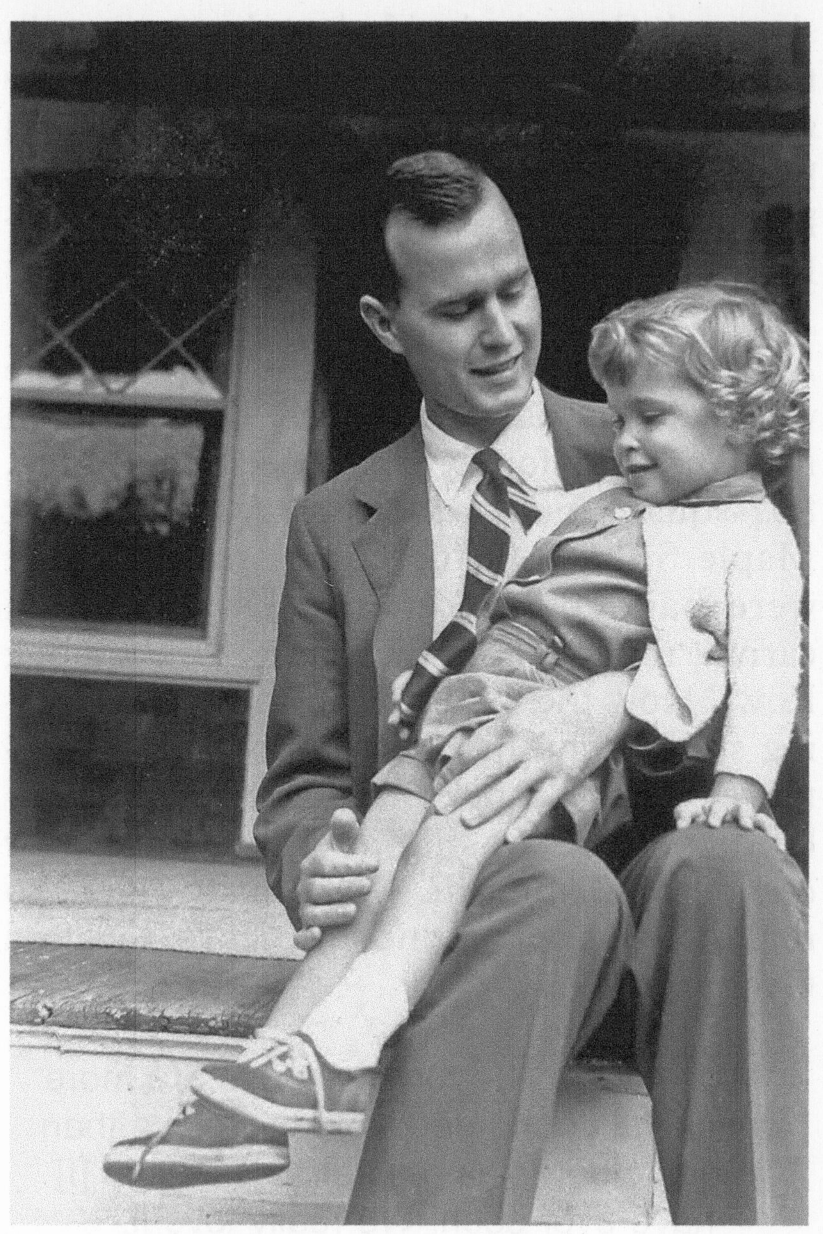

George and Robin.

funeral. It was too risky for the baby. Barbara never had a chance to say goodbye but she and George decided to honor her in their own way. On December 20, 1949, they welcomed a baby girl with blond hair and hazel eyes to the family. Her name was Pauline Robinson Bush. They would call her Robin.

After barely a year in California, George was needed back in Texas, this time in Midland. The family purchased a light blue, 847-square-foot house for $8,000 on East Maple Street. All the homes on the street were painted in soft pastel hues, which earned the block its nickname, "Easter Egg Row." Now the 1950s, even more enterprising spirits, who had heard about the potential of Texas oil fields, had arrived in Midland. "There wasn't anything subtle or complicated about it. We all just wanted to make a lot of money quick," recalled George.

> "Midland is a fine town — there are more congenial young people in this place than in any other town of near its size that [I] have ever seen. We really love it."
>
> — GEORGE BUSH WROTE HIS FRIEND GERRY BEMISS ON JANUARY 1, 1951.

Marvin Pierce flew to Texas to see where

the Bushes had decided to put down roots and raise their family. He didn't like that they were so far from home. *I worry about you,* admitted Marvin after a long flight from New York while he stood in the sand-blown neighborhood his daughter claimed to love. *What if something happened? Who would support you?* Barbara assured her father that they were surrounded by a sympathetic community. "We were all in the same situation. No one had any family. We were all newcomers and we came from all over the country. We formed really good friendships," she said.

The Bushes fit right in. Barbara joined the Midland Service League, volunteered at the local hospital, and both George and Barbara taught at Sunday school. After church, the neighborhood gathered for informal cookouts on their tiny patios swapping locations as well as potluck responsibilities. Out of the plains of West Texas a community grew.

In 1956, at age thirty-two, George was named one of Five Outstanding Young Texans of 1956. The *Midland Reporter-Telegram* wrote on Sunday, December 30, 1956:

Bush is a director of the Commercial Bank and Trust Company and is a director of the Independent Petroleum Association of America, serving as a member of its Imports Policy Committee. Bush has served as president of the Midland County Chapter of the American Cancer Society; helped to establish a foundation to benefit leukemia research; headed the general division of Midland's 1954 Community Chest Drive; was a founder of the Midland YMCA; served as youth trainer for the Midland Junior Baseball Association; served as director of the Midland Community Theater, and is chairman of the theater's building fund. He is a member of the Exchange Club, has served as Republican precinct chairman and in 1956 headed the Eisenhower-Nixon campaign fund drive in Midland County. Bush is a deacon and Sunday School teacher in the First Presbyterian Church and is a member of a committee in charge of the church's every-member canvass.

After two and a half years at Dresser, George made the difficult decision of leaving that path that had been so thoughtfully plotted by Neil Mallon to start a company with his neighbor, John Overbey. The poten-

Cookout in Midland.

Backyard get-together in Midland.

tial of a private venture was too enticing not to try and they formed Bush-Overbey Oil Development Co., Inc., a royalty company that required travel all over the United States.

The Bushes still flew to Kennebunkport in the summer for fresh air and to introduce their children to the tradition, but West Texas became their own. Everything they had created was built by them and even after pleasant visits to the northeast with family, they were happy to return to West Texas. George was even excited to return to work: "It is nice to be back in a way and the desk is stacked high with things to do," he wrote his uncle, Herbie Walker, on August 22, 1951. "This business is so darned exciting that when away for a little while only[,] many new developments have taken place."

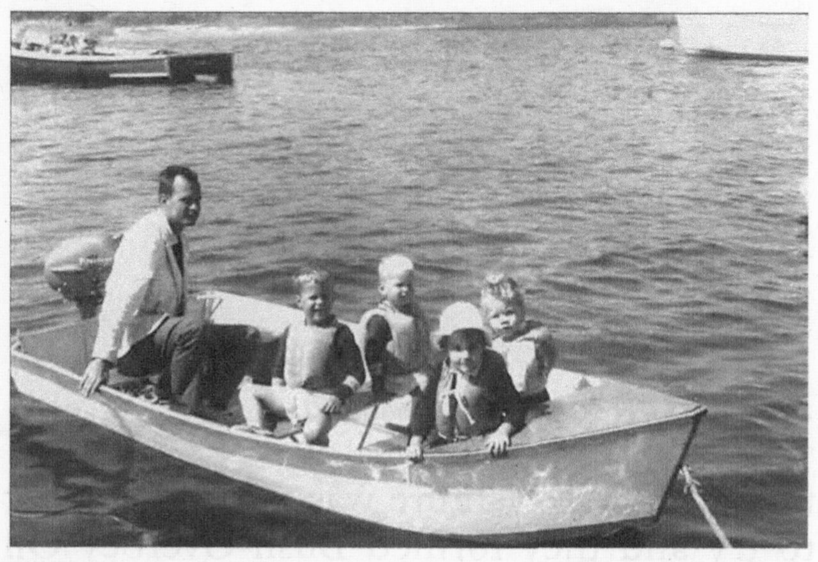

George with kids on boat in Kennebunkport.

With friends in Kennebunkport.

Until 1953, the Bush-Overbey operation was running smoothly, but they were looking to expand when two brothers, Bill and Hugh Liedtke, two independent oil operators, proposed the four join forces. Zapata Petroleum was incorporated later that year and was on its way to becoming a million-dollar company.

George's business was succeeding while Barbara ran the house. Together they continued to immerse themselves in the local community and formed a close circle of friends. They bought a larger home at 1412 West Ohio Avenue, which was three miles away from their old neighborhood and closer to George's office in downtown Midland. On February 11, 1953, their third child John

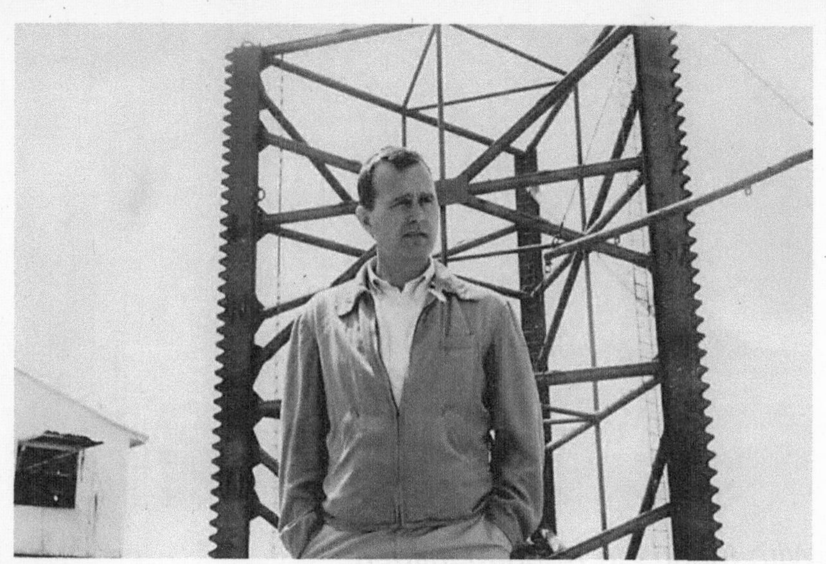

George near oil rig.

"Jeb" Ellis Bush was born.

West Texas seemed to be keeping her promises.

Fourteen: Friends, Faith, and Family

Three-year-old Robin wasn't acting like herself. Typically playful and fun, she was lethargic, withdrawn, and told her mom she was weighing the option of lying in bed all day. After a check-up and a few tests, the family pediatrician, Dr. Dorothy Wyvell, called Barbara and asked her to come back to the office, this time without Robin but with George.

In her office, Dr. Wyvell delivered the tragic news to the Bushes. *Your daughter has leukemia,* she said. Barbara and George, who were twenty-three and twenty-four at the time, had never heard of the disease. *Well, let's do something. What do we do?* pressed George. The doctor told them that there was nothing they could do. *There is no cure.*

"[Dr. Wyvell] gave us the best advice anyone could have given, which of course we didn't take," remembered Barbara. "She said, 'Number one, don't tell anyone. Number two, don't treat her. You should take her home, make life as easy as possible for her, and in three weeks' time, she'll be gone.' "

Refusing to accept those conditions, George and Barbara were on a plane with Robin the next day heading for Memorial Sloan-Kettering hospital in New York City. George's uncle was a doctor there, and he said they could try a few experimental treatments, bone marrow tests, blood transfusions, and chemotherapy. The doctors couldn't make any promises, but George and Barbara had to do something.

> "I remember asking the doctor why this was happening to our little girl, this perfectly beautiful creature. And the doctor said, 'You have to realize that every well person is a miracle. It takes billions of cells to make up a person. And all it takes is one cell to be bad to destroy a whole person.' So I came to see that the people who are sitting around alive are the miracles."
>
> — BARBARA BUSH

Barbara stayed by Robin's bedside in New York City while friends took care of Jeb and George W. back home. George traveled back and forth between the hospital and Texas. Somewhere in the haze of the diagnosis and the hospital bed in New York, Barbara accepted that Robin's life was out of her hands and placed in the able ones of the doctors and nurses. In this world, she was useless, but she could control her daughter's emotions, her comfort, and she could shoo away any scary thoughts. She read to her, made her laugh, brushed her hair, and assured her that there was nothing to worry about. "I wouldn't allow anybody to cry near her, so I'd have to say to [Dorothy] and [George], 'you can't come in the room if you're going to cry.' " George couldn't help his eyes filling with tears as he talked to his daughter or watched the process of the painful bone marrow tests. At Barbara's wish, he stepped into the hall to compose himself.

Robin died on October 11, 1953.

All of the strength that Barbara had assembled crumbled all at once when she felt the sting of her daughter's absence. The house in Texas was missing someone, and she fell asleep sobbing as George held her in their bed. "I fell totally apart and [George] took care of me. I cried every night," she said. Many relationships break after losing a child. "It either pulls you closer together or not." George and Barbara were patient with each other's grief. For all the strength Barbara had while Robin was alive, George found for Barbara after Robin had died. "George didn't let me retreat," she said.

When George was at work, Barbara played with George W. and cared for Jeb, trying to outrun the sadness. She knew she had to learn to live with her grief when it started to affect her little boys. One day back in Midland, there was a knock at the door; one of George W.'s friends was asking him to play. "He said out the window, 'I can't come out and play, I have to play with my mother.' That made me think I'm not doing this correctly," said Barbara.

The Bushes trudged forward, carrying the weight of their loss. George tucked a gold medallion into his wallet inscribed with "For the Love of Robin." Dorothy Bush had an oil painting commissioned of Robin. She's angelic and smiling with a twinkle in her eye in her frilly pink dress. George and Barbara hung it over the mantle in their Midland living room, so that Robin's memory would surround them as their family grew. Neil was born on January 22, 1955, and Marvin was born on October 22, 1956. The house was full of rowdy boys, train sets,

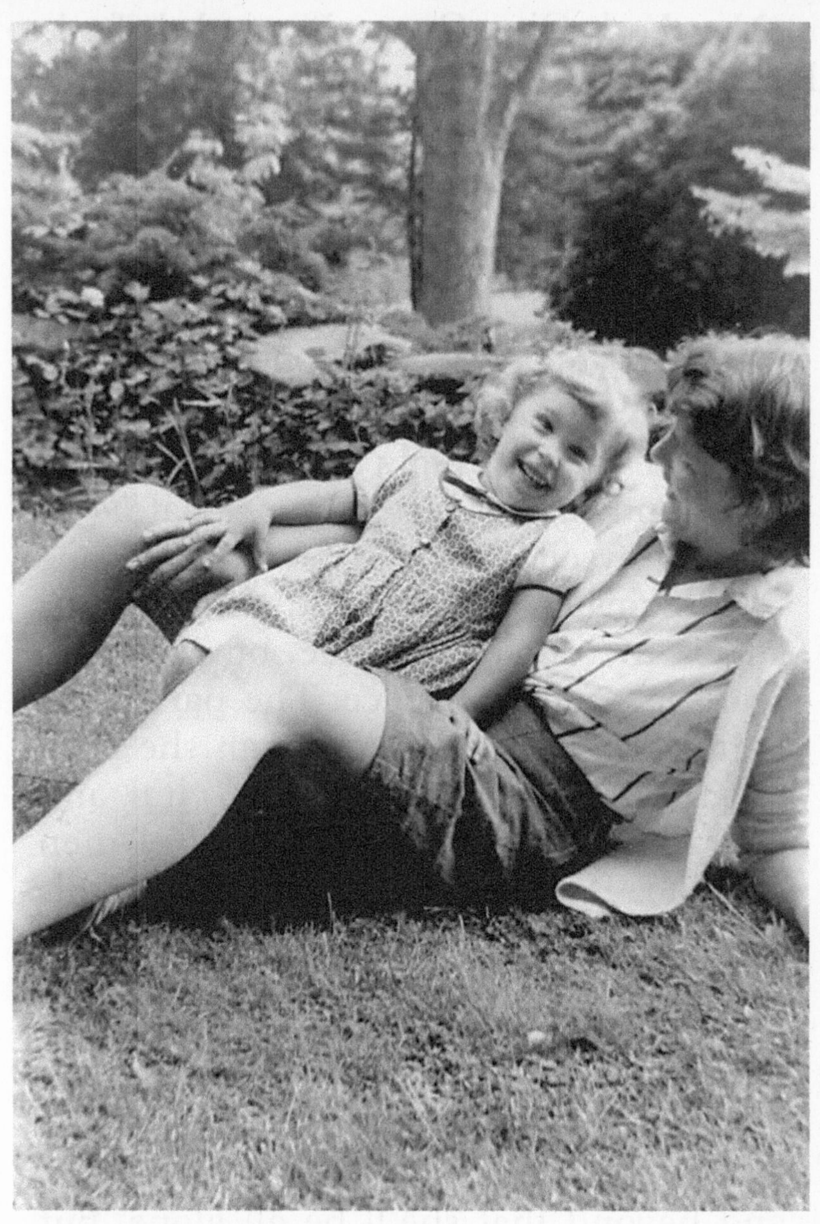

Barbara and Robin.

makeshift forts, and cowboy hats.

Five years later, while on a business trip

in New York City, George's mind drifted to Robin:

> Dear Mum,
> I have jotted down some words about a subject dear to your heart and mine. It is fun to fool around and try in one form or another to express thoughts that suddenly come up from way down deep in one's heart. Last night I went out on the town and on my way home — late — I said to myself, 'You could well have gone to Greenwich tonight' . . . this thought struck me out of the blue, but I felt no real sense of negligence. The part I like is to think of Robin as though she were a part, a living part, of our vital and energetic and wonderful family of men and Bar. Bar and I wonder how long this will go on. We hope we will feel this genuine closeness when we are 83 and 82. Wouldn't it be exciting at that age to have a beautiful 3 1/2 year-old daughter . . . she doesn't grow up. Now she's Neil's age. Soon she'll be Marvin's — and beyond that she'll be all alone, but with us, a vital living pleasurable part of our day-to-day life. I sometimes wonder whether it is fair to our boys and to our friends to 'fly-high' the portrait of Robin

which I love so much; but here selfishness takes over because every time I sit at our table with candlelight, I somehow can't help but glance at this picture you gave us and enjoy a renewed physical sensation of closeness to a loved one.

This letter . . . is kind of like a confessional . . . between you and me, a mother and her little boy — now not so little but still just as close, only when we are older, we hesitate to talk from our hearts quite as much.

There is about our house a need. The running, pulsating restlessness of the four boys as they struggle to learn and

Bucky, Jeb, Neil, George, and George W. in Midland.

George and Barbara with their four boys.

grow; the world embraces them . . . all this wonder needs a [counterpart]. We need some starched crisp frocks to go with all our torn-kneed blue jeans and helmets. We need some soft blond hair to offset those crew cuts. We need a doll house to stand firm against our forts and rackets and thousand baseball cards. We need a cut-out star to play alone while the others battle to see who's 'family champ.' We even need someone . . . who could sing the descant to 'Alouette,' while outside they scramble to catch the elusive ball aimed ever roofward, but usually thudding against the screens.

We need a legitimate Christmas angel — one who doesn't have cuffs beneath the dress.

We need someone who is afraid of frogs.

We need someone to cry when I get mad — not argue.

We need a little one who can kiss without leaving egg or jam or gum. We need a girl.

We had one once — she'd fight and cry and play and make her way just like the rest. But there was about her a certain softness.

She was patient — her hugs were just a little less wiggly.

Like them, she'd climb in to sleep with me, but somehow she'd fit.

She didn't boot and flip and wake me up with pug nose and mischievous eyes a challenging quarter-inch from my sleeping face.

No — she'd stand beside our bed till I felt her there. Silently and comfortable, she'd put those precious, fragrant locks against my chest and fall asleep.

Her peace made me feel strong, and

so very important.

'My Daddy' had a caress, a certain ownership which touched a slightly different spot than the 'Hi Dad' I love so much.

But she is still with us. We need her and yet we have her. We can't touch her, and yet we can feel her.

We hope she'll stay in our house for a long, long time.

Love,
Pop

By 1959, the four owners of Zapata decided to split into two separate companies and George took over the off-shore business, which operated in the Gulf of Mexico and eventually around the world. The new venture excited George — he would be on the water again. It also meant the family had to move. "We loved our life in Midland but there was one problem: Midland is nowhere near the Gulf of Mexico, where all our drilling rigs were operating. So a very pregnant Barbara, myself, and four boys packed up and moved to Houston," recalled George.

On August 18, 1959, a girl was born into the Bush clan, Dorothy Walker Bush. She was sweet and small with brown locks. They

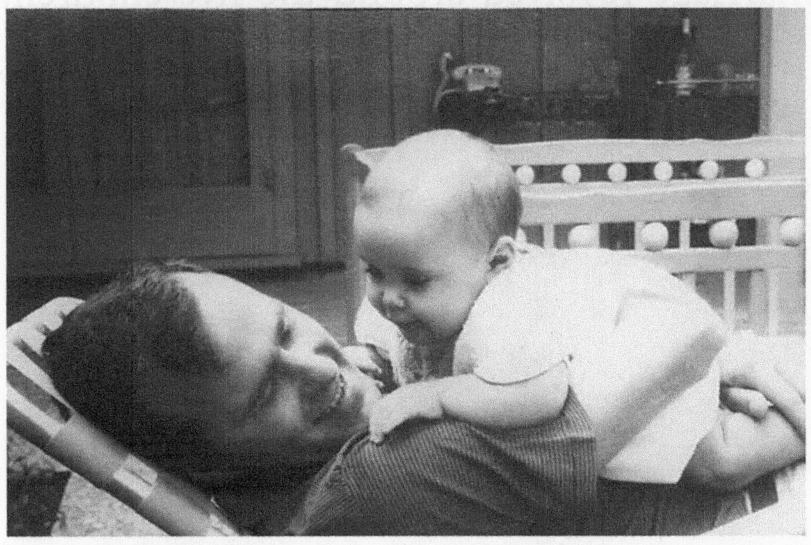

George and Doro.

would call her Doro.

For the next few years, the Bushes' calendars were color-coded mosaics of school pickups, baseball games, birthday parties, and George's departures and arrivals from business trips. "I spent half of the next ten years doing what every mother in America does: taxiing children to the doctor, the dentist, birthday parties, baseball games, tennis matches, and so on," recalled Barbara.

Barbara became the disciplinarian, or as the children remember: The Enforcer. She set the ground rules and watched her kids closely as they grew. George and Barbara's marriage revolved around the five children,

George, George W., and Barbara.

George and Doro playing football.

so did their house — they had a pool as well as a full baseball diamond made in the backyard.

A rushed letter from Barbara to her fam-

A growing family.

ily in October 1963 captures the essence of their days:

> "We have Ray and Harry Hoagland here for lunch today and Helen Healy. Then at 3:00 Neil and Marty go to a birthday party and at 4:00 Dorothy to another. Doro is going as the darndest witch you've ever seen. Tuesday 18 little boys (counting my own 3) will be here for a fried chicken din-

ner. Marty's 7th birthday. He is getting his first new bike–a 26 inch one. Very exciting. Wednesday night late we leave for the East and you all — Very exciting!"

In 2017, in Kennebunkport, their life and home again revolves around family. With marriages and births, the once small Bush family that fit inside a Midland home has expanded. Now there are great-grandkids to watch grow. Every flat surface of the turquoise living room is covered with framed family photographs. Each ordinary plastic frame faces the room for visitors to see.

Every summer, friends and family come

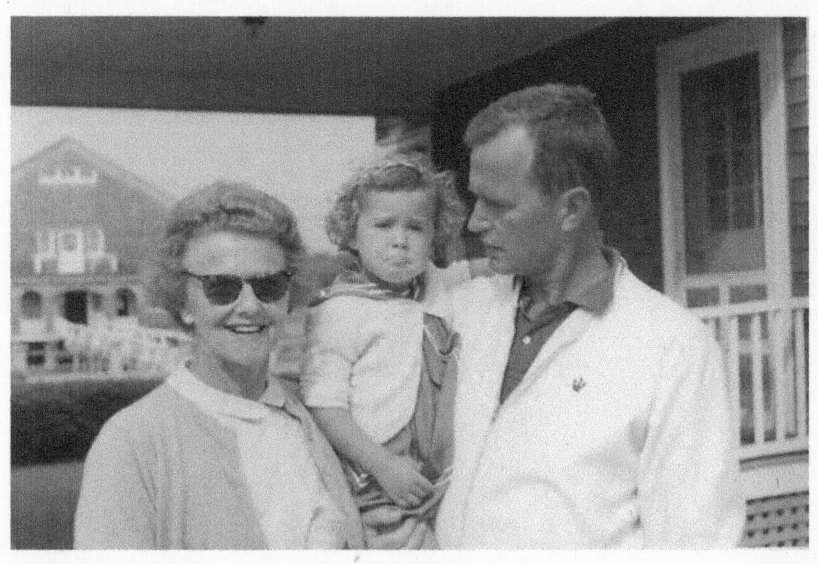

Dorothy, Doro, and George at Kennebunkport.

to Maine to visit; George and Barbara take their repeated arrivals as indicators of success. "[George] thinks it's a sense of humor that keeps us together, I don't think so; I think it's a love of family. I think his greatest accomplishment is . . . that our family comes up [to Maine] . . . [The children and grandchildren] are all a great example of what kept our marriage going. All the children coming up," she said.

Ganny and Gampy have both been a source of support and strength to me my entire life. In the fall of 2007, I was a junior in college. I won't bore you with the details but long story short it was a tough semester for me. By the time I went home for Christmas, I was very down on myself. "In the dumps," if you will. Not many people knew what was going on in my life, not even my closest friends, but I knew I could count on Ganny and Gampy to understand. I called my grandfather but he was away. In return, I got this letter which, still today, means the absolute world to me.

December 3, 2007

Dear Special Wonderful Ellie,
Your mom told me you tried to call me and she told me what it was about. My message back to you is that I love you, I am proud of you and I will always be in your corner. We all hit bumps in the road of life but you will get past this bump and go on to great things.

Here are some 'worry beads.' If you ever worry, rub these beads and the worries should fade away. Also, you can pawn them if you go broke in Tanzania.

For, as Doro once asked, "Are they real?" Well they are, so if you need a Starbucks double latte mocha special, peddle them.

One last point — if you ever need a shoulder to cry on, an arm to lift you up in the years ahead, or just plain someone to say "I love you, Ellie," I'm "da man." Also, if you need a back to rub, I am "da man." And I pay folding green.

Good luck in your fascinating life ahead. Out of difficulties come new exciting challenges. You will do well, of that I am sure.

Devotedly,
Gampy

FIFTEEN: OFF THEY GO!

"You have never known such a schedule as Pop has."
— BARBARA, WRITING TO HER FAMILY IN OCTOBER 1963

It was always in the back of their minds. George and Barbara knew they were heading toward a life in politics. While in Midland, they both volunteered during the Eisenhower and Nixon campaigns in 1952 and 1956.

George and Barbara watched Prescott and Dorothy's trajectory from afar. Prescott served as the U.S. Senator from Connecticut from 1952 to 1963. In the scrapbooks at the George Bush Presidential Library and Museum, next to photographs of kids growing up and life in Texas are carefully trimmed newspaper clippings about Prescott's votes and opinions. There are collections of Dorothy's influence too as the wife of a senator; she was graceful and opened up to the public about her life in D.C. with a weekly column that was printed in seventeen Connecticut newspapers. Prescott Bush was George's most influential mentor. "Wherever I was, whatever I did, he was the incentive behind everything," George wrote about his father after he died on October 8, 1972. When Barbara reflected on her relationship with Dorothy, she said: "I admired his mother more than anyone." So when George called Barbara in February 1962 to tell her that he wanted to run for the chairman of the Republican party of Harris County, she was not surprised.

He was elected chairman in 1963. At the time, Texas was a Democratic state, and while George had been advised by supportive friends to reconsider his party, he refused to change his views. "The argument made pragmatic sense, but I just couldn't see it. Philosophically I was a Republican, and the idea of a party switch didn't sit well with me," he said.

In 1963, George decided to run for the Senate, and he took on the incumbent Ralph Yarborough in the 1964 election. "Yarborough is diametrically opposed to almost everything I stand for. He is a 'federal interventionist.' He wants the government to do everything," George told the *Austin American* on October 12, 1963. And the race was on.

Barbara, who had attended George's campaign rallies when he was running for chairman, jumped on board. She'd find a spot either on stage or in the crowd, and she would needlepoint. She turned her projects into hand bags that read, "Bush," and "U.S. Senate" accompanied with an elephant, which became popularly known as "Bush Bags." "If George H. W. Bush is elected to the U.S. Senate in November,

George and Barbara in his office during the senate race.

historians of the future may give some of the credit to Mrs. Bush's needlepoint," claimed Teddye Clayton in the *Houston Post* on June 14, 1964. "Mrs. Bush, an energetic blonde, has hit where stickers and buttons and posters fall short — right on the feminine handbag."

George and Doro campaigning.

George and Barbara being interviewed.

> "It isn't exactly the way life used to be, but I enjoy it. It's all very exciting."
>
> — BARBARA BUSH, TO THE *HOUSTON POST* ON JUNE 14, 1964

George and Barbara were learning more about who they were and what they stood for politically. They began to realize that the listening, speaking, meeting, introducing, and socializing that was required of candidates came naturally. Together they became a powerful team.

Luckily, Barbara had help at home. After Doro was born, they hired Paula Rendon to watch over the children and to relieve Barbara of many household duties. What they didn't know at the time is Paula would be with them for the rest of their lives and she would become a cherished member of the Bush family. "What would I do without,

George and Barbara campaigning together during his bid for Congress.

Paula?" Barbara scribbled into her notebook after returning home from campaigning to a clean house and happy children.

Unlike George's oil business, politics allowed Barbara to become very involved and instrumental. She attended numerous rallies and even filled in for George when he could not make it to an event. In a letter home in September 1963, she wrote:

> I know from this meeting that I must go with Poppy whenever possible. First I can help him — if only to order sandwiches at the proper time 3 times a day. Secondly the candidate must be rescued often from the eager friend who has him cornered who starts off — "Let me tell you — —". I'll bet we had 150 different views on how we should act and what we should do. My conclusion of the whole affair is that we must be ourselves no matter what. I'm sure we'll get better as the months go by — no question there is lots of room for improvement. But I know I can help Pop. We are dropping the H.W. from our releases, etc. The big objection to Pop seems to be the Ivy League–Yankee label. I honestly can't worry about this too much for I feel sure that if he is seen and heard this will float out unimportant. How nice if

this were the only complaint! One of the many suggestions we had was that Pop don a cowboy hat for at least the country. I must say that I think this is lousy superficial advice. The main — big — thing I believe is to get around the state and get known. Not as a fake or a phony — but just get known as himself.

When their trips took them to Midland, they ran into old friends, which was a great comfort. "I love this part of campaigning," Barbara wrote to her family in November of 1963. She told them that a crowd of 350 people came to the school auditorium to hear George speak. "I cannot tell you how we felt seeing so many old friends. I could hardly stand it sitting on the stage. Terrible, but I had the most awful urge to wave like mad at everyone I saw. You will be pleased to know that I sat just as still as can be, and when George talked I never took my eyes off of him although I was in agony. Hopie Ritchie, Bobbie Hilliard, Toby, Brucie Ashmun, John and on and on. Let me put that differently: there must have been 20 people there we didn't know and love."

Of course, running for public office, George and Barbara entered into the spotlight and into a world of rumors and criticism. George was called a "carpetbagger" and an East Coast Ivy Leaguer who didn't belong in Texas. Barbara wrote her family about every twist, including one aimed at her in May 1964: "On arriving here last night we heard such a marvelous new one. In fact, saw it in writing from a lady (?) from Houston. 'Mrs. Bush is an heiress who spends all her time on the Cape.' I have never, to my knowledge, set my foot on the Cape, but vicariously I am enjoying my riches. Can you stand the stories!"

> "Bush's unique appeal is especially evident in neighborhoods where a lot of ambitious and fairly well-to-do young marrieds (25 to 40) live. There you hardly see a car these days that does not sport a Bush bumper sticker and many front lawns are decorated with small posters bearing his handsome likeness."
>
> — NEW YORK HERALD TRIBUNE

Even after a fierce and energetic campaign, George lost to Yarborough. The Bushes fell back into their Houston life, but somewhere along the campaign trail his ambitions for a life in public office had been realized. His next shot for a Washington post came in November 1966, this time for the

House of Representatives.

Barbara's unwavering loyalty that she would later become known for set in early and naturally as did George's ambitions for higher offices. She wrote to a friend on January 6, 1966:

> The days are getting closer to Feb. 7th and George has not made up his mind to run. The whole thing has been complicated by that funny Ross Baker. We kept hearing that Ross was going to run. Pop finally went by to see Ross the other day. Ross said that he was going to run and nobody could change his mind. George told him all the reasons why he felt that a primary between two friends with the same beliefs would hurt the party, but Ross said that he felt he could beat Pop and that in any case a primary was healthy for the party. Tom Thawley was here just before Christmas and he had talked to Ross. I got mad at Tom (quietly) because he not only didn't discourage Ross, but he seemed to feel that the fact that Ross only wanted to be a congressman and not move up to the senate was in Ross's favor. Later when Pop went to see Ross, Ross said just that. Pop said, 'I don't want to move just up to the senate, Ross. I'd like to be President. The

chances are slight, but please don't limit me.' Ross also told Pop that no one had urged him to run, although friends have told him that if he does it they will support him. Can you imagine running with no urging? Uggh!

Leaving Zapata was a difficult choice for George. The senate race taught him campaigning was a full-time job and he had a difficult decision ahead. Barbara wrote George W. at Andover on January 25, 1966:

Dearest George,
Not much news of interest to you, but I do feel that you should know that we still care. And believe me, brother, we do. Our life has gotten to a really [emotional] [crossroads] for Dad. If the deal goes through that he is working on, we will no longer be part of Zapata. I feel sure that at your age this does not seem as emotional an issue that it is at our age. Dad has spent a lot of time this week thinking back over his years with Zapata, all the people who have made it a success and feeling a little overcome with gratitude to the people who have [made] our lives so easy etc. This is quite a move for Dad and he has thought long

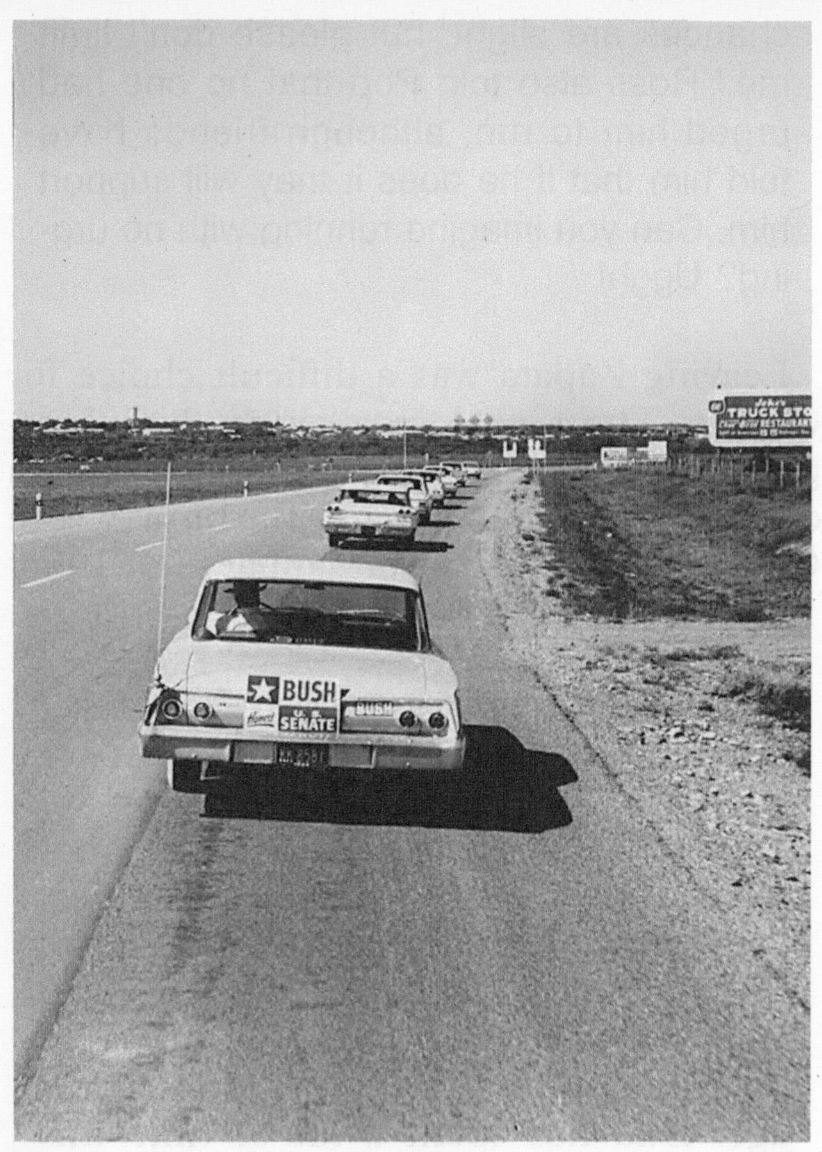

Bush for Senate bumper sticker.

and hard about giving up his job. He will devote himself to the campaign from now to the fall and then decide after the election what he wants to do. I do

Cheering George on at a rally.

believe that he will go around the world this spring — or at least try to go to Vietnam and the Far East. This will be very helpful to him in the fall. It is almost impossible to talk about the problems without seeing them yourself. Meanwhile he is now trying to get an organization set up here.

George went all in. He left Zapata in

George and Barbara campaigning.

February 1966. "I resigned as chairman and CEO of Zapata to devote full time to running for Congress. It would have been unfair to the company's stockholders and employees to do otherwise. The 1964 Senate race taught me that it takes a total com-

George and Barbara after his win.

mitment to be a candidate. Zapata, like any successful business, needed hands-on leadership from its front office," explained George.

In a note written on January 15, 1966, Barbara wrote how her youngest was absorbing the campaign:

> "George announced on Sat. January 15 that he was a candidate for the 7th Congressional seat. Monday morning I was taking Doro's carpool when I heard one little girl say to Doro 'I saw your Daddy on television last night.' Another child said 'You did, What was he doing?' And Doro answered 'Oh you know it was about that erection that he is going to have.' Needless to say we have worked on the word election!"

On November 8, 1966, George won the election, and the Bushes were on their way to Washington, D.C.

It was early fall of 1992 and I was in kindergarten at Westbrook Elementary School in Bethesda, Maryland. My classmates and I were in art class, painting on large easels. I was a normal five-year-old little girl, or so I thought. One of my classmates, whose name I will not name, sauntered over from her easel to mine and whispered to me: "I hope your grandfather loses the race." Even at five, I felt a surge of love and pride for my grandfather and somewhere deep down something took over. I dipped my paintbrush in red and painted a stripe down her face.

Bush family members are fiercely loyal and supportive of each other. Sometimes this means a shoulder to lean on or a hand to hold during a tough time. Sometimes it means defending someone in the press. And other times this has meant giving up part of your life to work tirelessly on the campaign trail. All of our family members have done this for my grandfather, my uncles, and my cousin George P. It's what we do!

My earliest "memory" of campaigning was for my grandfather in 1988. I was two years old and a star in one of his most popular presidential advertisements. The ad opens with me running across the lawn in Maine and running into my grandfather's arms and ends with a big kiss from my grandfather.

As the years went on, my brother and I spent lots of time with my grandparents on the campaign trail. I remember traveling around the United States by train with my grandparents on their "Spirit of America" tour as my grandfather ran for his second term as president. My role was easy: hang out with my grandparents, maybe wave to some supporters. Looking back, I'd like to think that we acted as a source of comfort for my grandparents who were working tirelessly day in and day out toward a common goal.

When I was a freshman in high school, I recruited six of my closest friends to join me in Colorado for the "Youth for George W. Bush" campaign push. They needed young people out there to help get the vote. We spent days going door to door through Boulder, Colorado. I would start off with "Hello, my name is Ellie and I hope you will vote for my uncle George W. Bush for president!" At times, we had doors closed in our faces and unkind words thrown our way.

Four years later, during the summer between high school and college, my cousin Marshall and I worked at the George W.

Ellie holding a sign in support of her Gampy.

Bush for President campaign headquarters in Arlington, Virginia. It was my first real 9-to-5 job and I loved every minute. I spent long days greeting guests, sorting mail, and making campaign calls. Just like the doors slamming in our faces, we had plenty of angry people slamming the phones in our ears.

It was all worth it, though. If anyone else in my family decides to run for office, whatever it may be, I will be there for them, no question.

SIXTEEN:
DIVING HEAD-FIRST INTO THE WORLD OF POLITICS

"I love people, and I guess that's all politics is."

— BARBARA BUSH

For the next four years, George and Barbara would prove that they were very good at making friends.

George and Barbara moved to the District of Columbia in January 1967 with three children in tow: Neil, Marvin, and Doro. George W. was at Yale in New Haven, and Jeb wanted to finish junior high at Kinkaid in Houston, so he stayed with friends. The family settled into an old house on Hillbrook Lane, which they bought from Senator Milward Simpson of Wyoming. The home had more problems than charm. "One day I came downstairs to find George sitting in the living room under an umbrella," remembered Barbara. "A bathtub had leaked right through the ceiling." A year

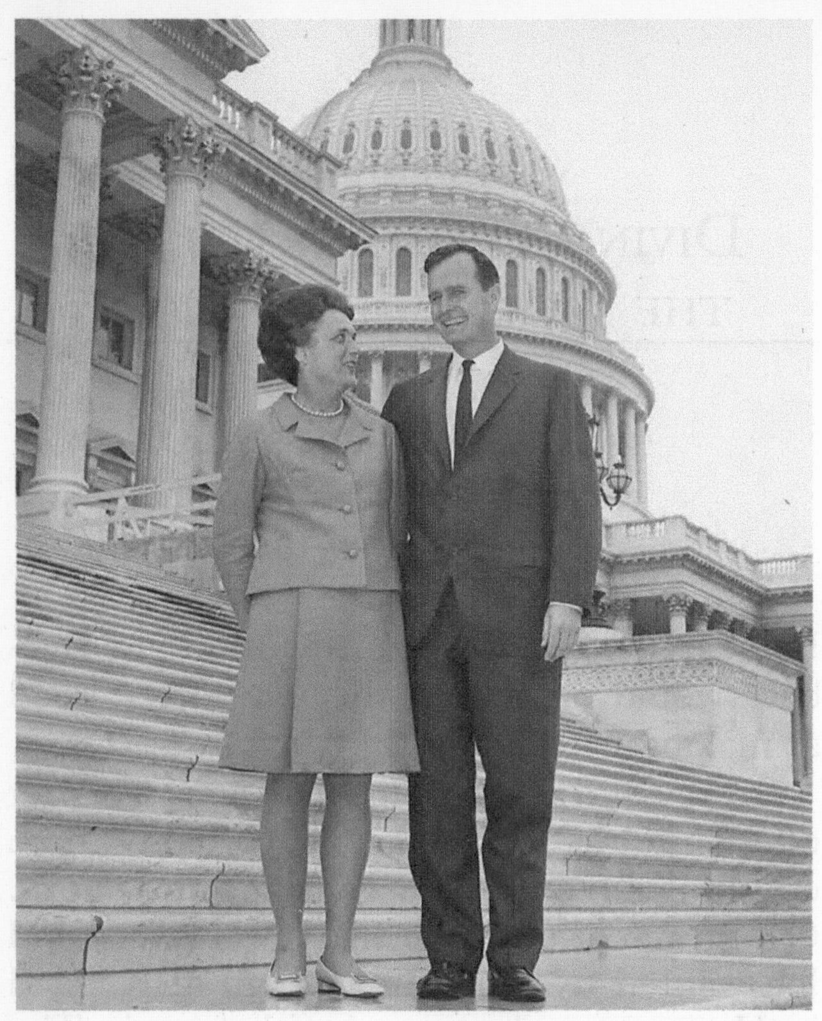

Barbara and George in Washington.

later, they moved to Palisade Lane and into a four-story brick townhouse, which felt more like home, and they would own it for a decade.

George got to work. He was appointed to serve on the Ways and Means Committee, becoming the first freshman congressman to do so in over sixty years. Because of the distinction, George was invited to a lot of events. He was also chairman of the House Republican Research Committee Task Force on Earth Resources and Population. In his first year in Congress, George visited eleven provinces in Vietnam, where he spoke with generals, soldiers, and civilians on the ground. He would later vote to abolish the draft and support American withdrawal from Vietnam.

> "This was a very interesting time to be living in Washington. The Vietnam War was debated at all the dinner parties, and the whole country worried about racial and student unrest."
>
> — BARBARA BUSH

While in office, George received over a thousand letters regarding the Fair Housing Act of 1968, which turned out to be his most controversial stance — at least in the eyes of many Texans, who opposed the bill. While George claimed to be against the legislation when he ran for senate in 1964, he voted in favor of it as a congressman. The bill passed and was signed into law in April of 1968. After his vote, George received hate mail and threats. Back in Houston, he decided to face the outrage at an open meeting.

Boos and yells bounced off the walls of the high school gym, but George stood his ground. "What this bill does do in this area

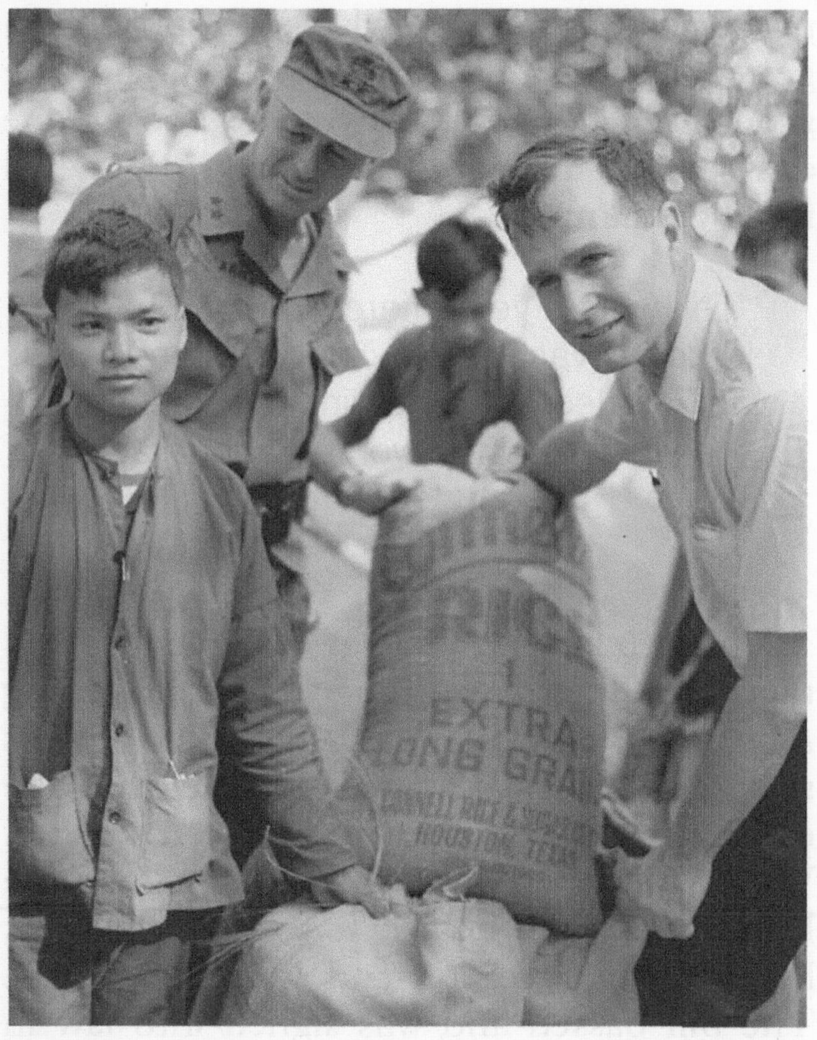

George's trip to Vietnam.

is to remove an obstacle — what it does do is try to offer a promise of hope — a realization of The American Dream," said George, who argued if soldiers can fight in Vietnam, then they should be able to come home and find housing. "The door will not be slammed solely because he is a Negro, or because he speaks with a Mexican accent."

His passionate explanation of his stance seemed to have resonated with many. The *Houston Chronicle* reported: "Booed before the talk, he won a standing ovation by the end."

Barbara jumped into Washington life too. She attended events for the Congressional Wives Club, Washington Committee for the American Field Service, Urban Service Corps, International Club II (founded by Dorothy Bush), and Ladies Committee of the Smithsonian Institute. In her diary, she recorded her weekly engagements: luncheons with Capitol Hill wives, briefings at the State Department, talks that interested her, errands, then she'd race back to pick up the kids, help with homework and school projects, and then get dressed for a function in the evening with George.

Barbara exploring with the kids.

"You have to learn in Washington that you can't do everything. Like all of life, you have to set your priorities, and it took me a while to discover that."

— BARBARA BUSH

In his first term, George flew back to Houston often, leaving Barbara with the children on weekends. "It was a strange life, but an exciting one," recalls Barbara. She took the kids all over Washington, snapping photographs and absorbing its many sights. "History swallows one up here and I find myself bursting with pride over everything," she wrote in her diary on February 11, 1967. "Sad to say, this feeling has to remain a secret one. In a few minutes I am going to awaken Marvin and we will take off for another day of sightseeing. Our aim is to see the National Museum of Natural History. There is so much to see and I am eager to take the children to see a little every weekend . . ."

Her enthusiastic documentation would prove to be handy in later years when George ran for Senate again. She created her own presentation, "Little Known Places of Interest to Visit in Washington," and she brought her slides to school auditoriums, committee meetings, and other functions all over Texas.

Family time in Washington was packaged with work and often included politicians and community members. "Because Dad's schedule was jam-packed, Sundays took on an even greater importance to our family. It was when we went to church and had a Sunday lunch with the whole family and various friends and neighbors. The late congressman Sonny Montgomery, a Democrat from Mississippi, came over regularly. Supreme Court Justice Potter Stewart and his wife, Andy, lived on our street," recalled Doro Bush Koch in *My Father, My President.*

In the summer, after work and on the weekends, they'd take George's boat out on

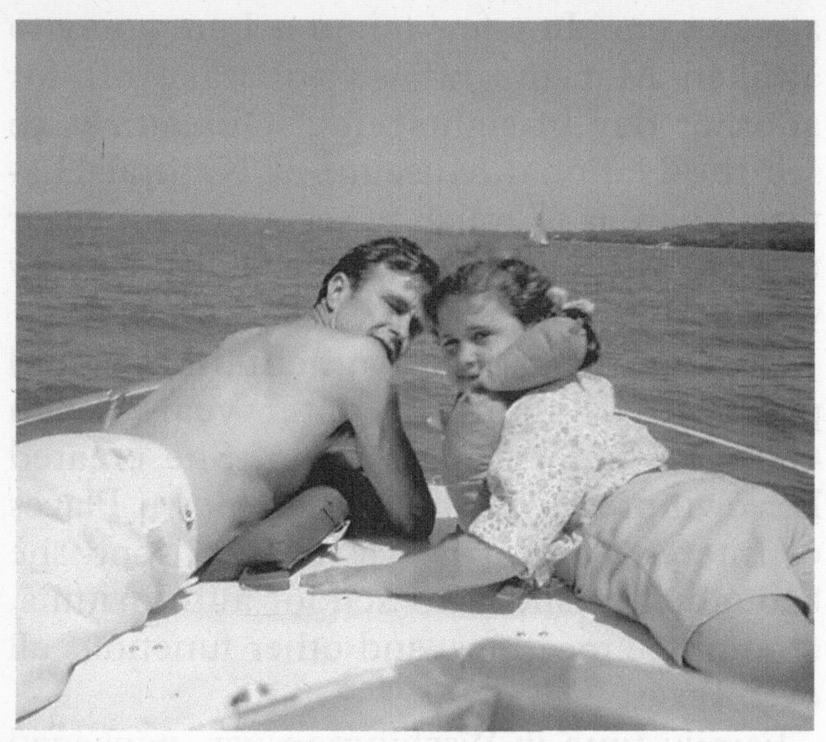

George and Doro on their boat.

the Potomac. Barbara would assemble a picnic for the guests and they'd anchor by the Lincoln Memorial to listen to the Army Band Concert. On Wednesday, July 19, 1967, a list notes that they had cheese and crackers, salad, Chinese noodles, creamed chicken, and cake on board. "Took Bill Cowger (Kentucky), John Paul Hammerschmidt (Arkansas), Sam Steiger (Arizona), Kitty and Ken Hall (State Department), Karen Kleinfelder [*Dallas Morning News*], G.H.W.B. and BPB. Great fun, ate at Mount

Vernon. Lovely night on the water."

When George and Barbara went to dinners, she jotted in her diary what the hosts served, how they decorated, who they invited; she was constantly monitoring luncheons and get-togethers gathering information on how to be successful in this social world.

While they were a determined pair, it wasn't an easy road for anyone. In her diary, Bar-

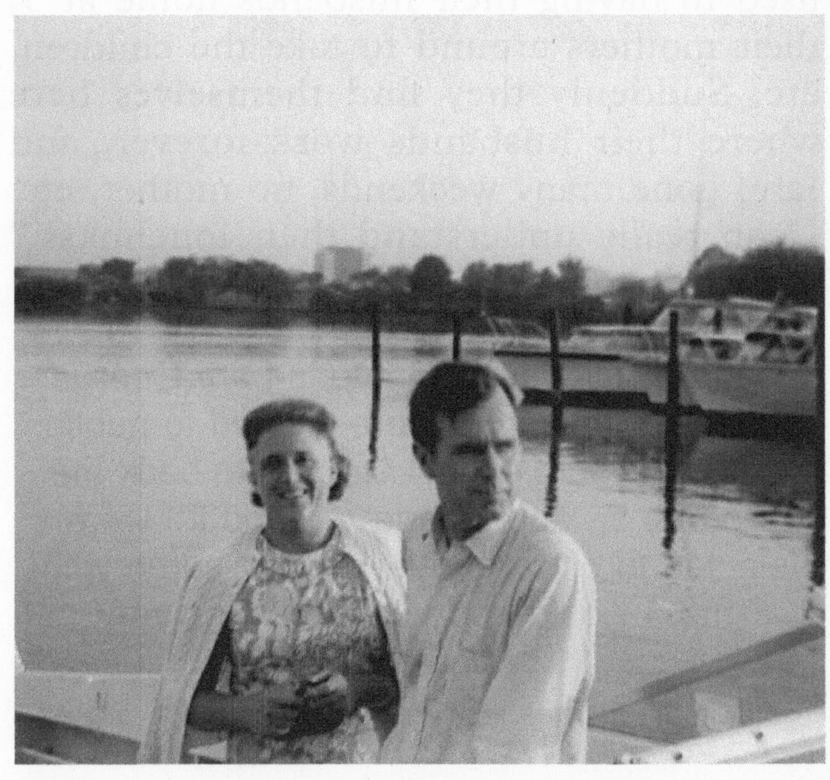

Barbara and George on the Potomac River.

bara noted separations and divorces, which were happening in their circles. "Ugh!! So sad," she would write in her diary, but she'd never spend too much time on the topic.

At teas and events, she'd hear from the younger congressman's wives who it wasn't easy on because they had young children and they were far from home. "I hear that a lot of our new wives are miserable, homesick and lonely. I feel very sorry for them. It usually is the young wives with young children who came from small towns. They were used to having their husbands home at 5, their mothers around to take the children, etc. Suddenly they find themselves here where their husbands work forever, and [are] gone many weekends, no mother, etc. I can really understand their loneliness," she wrote to a friend on April 20, 1967.

> "I know my claim to fame is I am George Bush's wife . . . If I were elected to public office, I would expect George to back me and be an appendage . . . and if I were elected to office and he did not agree with me, I would hope he'd be very, very quiet."
>
> — BARBARA BUSH

Every marriage has chapters, and this one

was all about politics. George was busy, distracted, and always on the move. It wasn't an easy path to navigate, but George and Barbara remained aligned. She knew his greater ambitions, and she did everything she could to support his journey. She told the *Dallas Morning News* that her main responsibility "is to hang in there as a wife and mother."

Of course, even in the hectic atmosphere of politics in Washington, celebrations are important. In January 1970, twenty-five years after saying "I do," George and Barbara drove to the Bayou Club in Houston, where Barbara was met with a large surprise party for their anniversary.

Later that same year, George had been convinced to run for senate again. Yarborough looked vulnerable, and President Richard Nixon and his administration thought George could take him on. However, a predicament that no one saw coming, Yarborough was beat in the primaries by Democrat Lloyd Bentsen. The race against Bentsen was close — 53.5 to 46.5 — but George would be out of a job in 1971. Another defeat hurt, but George did not seem to give up hope.

Nixon, who had encouraged George to

run, offered the Texan a position as the assistant to the president, but George had something else in mind. He argued that he would be the most sensible and effective U.S. Ambassador to the United Nations. Nixon was swayed. "My feelings are kind of mixed. I'll miss the Congress, but it's going to be a tremendously exciting new challenge," Bush recorded in his diary on December 11, 1970.

The Bushes were moving further north to New York City.

Barbara and George enjoying a moment of levity.

George and Barbara on plane.

Everything is grand about the forty-seven-story Waldorf-Astoria on Park Avenue in New York City. The building, designed in 1931, was at the time the world's largest hotel. Above the twenty-eighth floor are art deco–style private residences where many famous guests have resided, including the Duke and Duchess of Windsor, Frank Sinatra, and Elizabeth Taylor.

The luxury towers would be home to George, Barbara, and twelve-year-old Doro from 1971 until 1973. "At the time, it was home to Mrs. Douglas MacArthur; actress Carol Channing; former Senator Bill Benton; former postmaster general and confidant of Franklin Roosevelt, Jim Farley, with whom we shared several fun dinners; Mrs. Edwin Hilson, a great friend of the Eisenhowers; benefactress Mrs. Charles Engelhard; and many others," reported Barbara, who was slightly intimidated by the roster.

With armloads of groceries she wondered if this was the protocol — "Would somebody tell me that their clientele did not carry groceries up in the tower elevators, much less through the lobby?"

Of course it was fine.

George's main responsibility at the United Nations was to translate the vision and objectives of the administration. It was what he had pitched to Nixon to get the job in the first place. In Chief of Staff H.R. Haldeman's office, George explained: "I thought the U.N. would have some real appeal because I could spell out his programs with some style and we could preempt that mass new media area — that he was operating almost in a vacuum." While critics saw the role as inefficient, George felt he "could really put forward an image there that would be very helpful to the Administration."

"Our life in N.Y.C. is extraordinary! First of all it is very very busy. Secondly I have met the most exciting people. And thirdly — Pop is absolutely fascinated with the work — big four meetings, etc. and fifths. All Texans not only come to N.Y.C. but stay in our hotel! It is unbelievable. Our apartment (called an Embassy) is atop the Waldorf Towers — very big for a U.S. apartment — very small for a U.S. Embassy. But just right for us. We can easily seat 36 for dinner."

— BARBARA, TO A FRIEND IN 1971

Aside from the many parties and events and the interesting people they met and the things they learned about the world, the U.N. job turned out to be the challenge George was looking for. George's most difficult issue at the U.N. was executing the Nixon administration's "dual representation" policy for China. While Taiwan had a seat at the U.N., the People's Republic of China did not. When the vote came — 59 to 55 — that Taiwan was out and China was in, George, who had his "heart and soul wrapped up in the policy of keeping Taiwan from being ejected" was disappointed to see the Taiwanese government leave and felt "it was a dark moment for the United Nations and international diplomacy."

Despite the sting, the Bushes looked

forward and fulfilled their pledge to make new friends. Months later, George invited the Chinese delegation to Sunday lunch at the Bush family home on Grove Lane in Greenwich. The Minute Rice that Dorothy Bush prepared for the occasion sat in the oven for a lot longer than sixty seconds and the foreign minister asked what it was. "Poor Mom. The rice was so overcooked that even the Chinese did not recognize it," recalled Barbara.

On June 17, 1972, five men were caught breaking into the Watergate complex — the Democratic National Headquarters. The event (not yet dubbed the Watergate Scandal) began to make headlines across the United States — *who were they and why were they trying to bug the complex?* Even as allegations flew, the incident did not affect Nixon's reelection in November 1972.

After the election, Nixon invited George up to Camp David, where he asked him to head the Republican National Committee. George and Barbara were both caught off guard by the appointment. Barbara told George not to take it — she knew the weight of the task ahead and she worried that leaving the U.N. would hurt George's reputation. George wrote President Nixon:

Dear Mr. President,

. . . Frankly, your first choice for me came as quite a surprise particularly to Barbara. The rarefied atmosphere of international affairs plus the friendship in New York and the Cabinet seem threatening to her. She is convinced that all our friends in Congress, in public life, in God knows where — will say, 'George screwed it up at the U.N. and the President has loyally found a suitable spot.' "

In the letter, George continued that while he would accept the appointment as the Republican National Committee chairman, he really wanted the "Number 2" spot in the State Department. "My love affair is not with the State, it's with high-level policy dealings on international matters," he offered. But Nixon held his position on what was best for George — the R.N.C. — and he and Barbara and Doro moved back to Washington.

"George is all over the U.S.A. Needless to say Watergate does not help him *at all* but he has his great faith in the system and in the President!"

— BARBARA BUSH, IN HER DIARY ON MONDAY, JANUARY 14, 1974

It's true, George did not lose faith in the president until the very end. He spent most of his time defending the party and the administration. It's also true that he was all over the country. In 1973, with news conferences, speeches, and interviews on national television, George traveled close to 100,000 miles and visited thirty-three states in one year. "Mail poured into the RNC office, most of it from loyal Republicans. I spent an enormous amount of time as chairman trying to reassure them that our political system was sound, that the Republican National Committee, thus the party, had nothing to do with Watergate, and that our President was innocent," he wrote. "It was not an easy job."

> "I am worried about George as he does not love his work. How could he? All this scandal."
>
> — BARBARA BUSH, IN HER DIARY ON MONDAY, JANUARY 14, 1974

By 1974, the scandal had ripped through the White House. Top staffers began to resign and the Senate Watergate Committee began televised hearings. Still Nixon maintained his innocence and, therefore, George stood by him. As the role became more

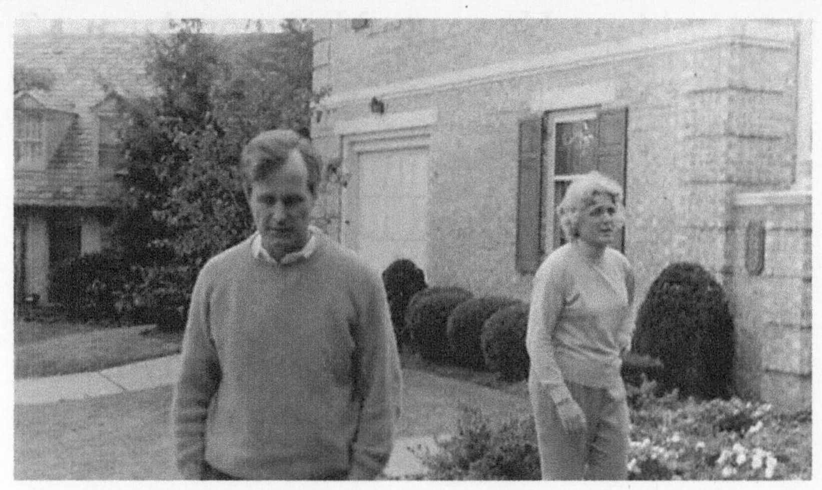

George and Barbara in Washington, D.C.

stressful, George's time with Barbara and the family was all the more sporadic, and he let his mind drift to happier places. He wrote to Barbara on July 24, 1974, "Now en route to Los Angeles (press conference) S.F. speech tonight. All I can really think about is the peace that I know when I am with you in Maine."

By the summer of 1974, the House Judiciary Committee had approved three articles of impeachment. Many called for Nixon's resignation. After a Cabinet meeting on August 6, 1974, in which the president refused to acknowledge the gravity of the charges — "The atmosphere was one of unreality," George recalled in his diary — George decided he could no longer defend the president. He wrote Nixon on August 7, 1974:

> "Dear Mr. President,
> It is my considered judgment that you should now resign. I expect in your lonely embattled position this would seem to you as an act of disloyalty from one you have supported and helped in so many ways . . ."

On August 9, 1974, Barbara and George went to the White House to watch Nixon resign and Vice President Gerald Ford take over. "There is no way to really describe the emotion of the day," George dictated to his diary on August 9, 1974. "Bar and I went down and had breakfast at the White House. Dean and Pat Burch and the Buchanans were there in the Conference Mess. There was an aura of sadness, like somebody died. Grief. Saw Tricia and Eddie Cox in the Rose Garden — talked to them on the way into the ceremony. President Nixon looked just awful. He used glasses — the first time I ever saw them. Close to breaking down — understandably. Everyone in the room in tears. The speech was vintage Nixon — a kick or two at the press — enormous strains. One couldn't help but look at the family and the whole thing and think of his accomplishments and then think of the shame and wonder what kind of a man is this really."

Seventeen: Distance, It's Good for the Heart

"I miss you more than tongue can tell, but maybe these gaps are good cause they teach me I could never live without you."
— GEORGE, TO BARBARA

George met with President Ford to advocate his candidacy for the vice presidency; however, Ford chose Nelson Rockefeller. Instead George asked to be Chief of the U.S. Liaison Office in China. All the kids were in school — Neil, nineteen, was at Tulane University, Marvin, eighteen, was a senior at Woodberry Forest School in Virginia, and Doro, fifteen, was going to boarding school at Miss Porter's School in Farmington, Connecticut. George W., twenty-six, was attending Harvard Business School. After studying abroad in Mexico, Jeb, twenty-one, met and fell in love with Columba Garnica Gallo from León. They married on February 23, 1974. Jeb graduated from the University of Texas at Austin, and he and Columba moved to Houston.

It seemed the ideal time for a new adventure. "The more George talked, the more excited I got," remembered Barbara. "I missed being with George — he had traveled a great deal as RNC chairman — and the thought of having him to myself sounded like the answer to my prayers." In October of 1974, they flew to China by way of Anchorage and Tokyo. The new family cocker spaniel, C. Fred, rode in the cargo; he was making the journey too.

The United States had yet to establish a formal ambassadorship to the People's Republic of China. There was a liaison office and George was determined to improve relationships with key government officials. He believed China — with a growing economy and one-fourth of the world's population — was an inevitable part of the future.

Before the Bushes took off, Barbara took language classes at the State Department, and they were briefed on cultural differences. "We have learned so many things in such a short time about China. I wonder just how true they will prove to be?!" Barbara scribbled into her notebook while on the plane on October 17, 1974. Her notes from her briefings included: "Don't hold

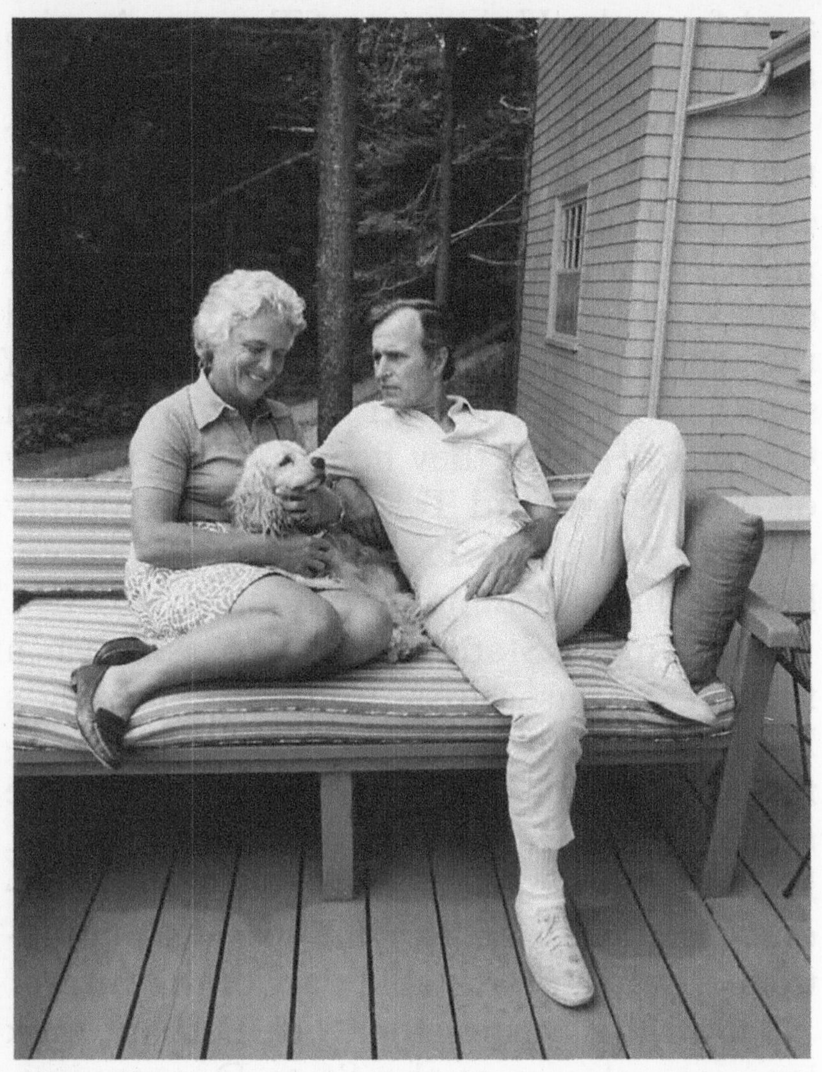

Barbara and George enjoying a moment of quiet with C. Fred.

hands with George. Don't touch the Chinese . . . never look at or mention Chinese women's feet . . . the Chinese are superstitious about the spout of a teapot pointing at anyone, always point the spout between people."

Flying over the Pacific Ocean, George and Barbara had no idea what to expect. It was a whole new world for both of them. On October 24, 1974, Barbara wrote to her good friend Andy Stewart while they were in the air over Shanghai: "All I saw of that city was the rice fields and the truck gardens from the air. They have the most beautiful fields — all colors of green and although there was a slight drizzle we could see 12 or 15 people working together in many fields." Because of the flat landscape they flew over and the unknown adventure ahead, they both began to recall that same exciting feel they had when they moved to West Texas. George wrote home to James Baker on November 17, 1974:

> "We're here. We have been for almost four fascinating weeks — weeks filled with a variety of emotions. This is a land of contrasts. Great beauty but also a lot of gray dirt and drabness. Clear (almost balmy) skies then fierce penetrating cold, urged on to ferocious heights by a North wind that reminds me of the West Texas winds, carrying a lot of real estate. Enormous beauty of the children with their

captivating smiles and robust healthy looks contrasted with a certain dreary sameness as one watches the workers cycling out of Peking [Beijing] to work in the AM and back from work in the PM. It's great and we are very happy here, though both Bar and I miss family, friends, news, even politics. It is funny how fast we get cut off . . ."

Citizens did not own private cars in Beijing; most people commuted via bicycle. In the morning and early evenings, the dirt roads were overflowing with a steady stream of cyclers. The Bushes decided to follow suit and bought two bikes, which they used often. They had a driver, but their preferred mode of transportation was also one way of making it clear — the Bushes' diplomacy was going to be different from predecessor David Bruce. Bruce had "felt it was best to have a small mission, keep a low profile," but George was trying to make real changes. "My hyper-adrenaline, political instincts tell me that the fun of this job is going to be to try to do more, make more contacts," George told his diary in October 1974. To George, that meant attending National Day celebrations for other embassies, something previous diplomats had never done. On

November 1, 1974, George and Barbara showed up to the Algerian National Day. "The Algerian ambassador looked like he was going to fall over in a dead faint when he saw us arrive," said George.

George and Barbara visiting Soochow.

Despite George's increased efforts to make friends in Beijing, the job was far less grueling than his round-the-clock position as R.N.C. chairman. Barbara enjoyed the change. Not just the freedom of biking around to interesting places every day but also the added time with her husband. "Back in Washington or at the United Nations the telephone was ringing all the time. George would come home and say, excuse me, and pick up the phone. It's very different here," Barbara told Don Oberdorfer of the *Washington Post* in December 1974. "In his first five weeks I think he received two telephone calls, except for the ones from me. I try to call him once a day. I think he misses the phone as much as anything."

Barbara wrote home on March 5, 1975: "I love being included in on these business trips with George and will sit through hours of the stilted conversations and the endless cups of green tea that one must drink on these occasions."

In the mornings and at night, they walked C. Fred, which attracted many stares from locals. Barbara had decided to master the phrase *Ni bu pa. Ta shi shau go. Ta bu yau ren.* (Don't be afraid. He's a little dog. He doesn't bite people.)

When the wind wasn't blowing too hard,

Barbara in the Forbidden City.

they would go for long rides. Barbara wrote home in November 1974:

> "We rode one day into the southern part of town, paid an ancient lady a few pennies and put our bikes in a bike parking lot. We walked up a tiny little street that used to be the old theater district and is now filled with tiny specialty shops. Nothing fit for Park or Fifth Avenues, but shops with hats, clothes, food, etc. We were the only westerners that we saw for two hours. It was great fun and Pop bought a red drum that he claimed he'd always wanted. He tied it on his bike and rode home with it. We are getting used to being stared at.

Every place we go people stare and stare. I mean a foot or two from your face. Sometimes I smile and speak to them and they sometimes answer, but most often go into gales of laughter."

For Christmas, George and Barbara made the difficult decision to spend the holiday apart. She wrote the kids on November 18, 1974: "The minute you all get tucked back into school, I am going to fly back to Dad. I have been so spoiled and can hardly bare to think of being away from him that long." George had felt the same and on December 4, 1974, he recorded in his diary:

"Great talks with Bar on the phone. The kids all doing fine. It is as if each one of these five kids, recognizing that the family was undergoing a different experience, are pulling together much more. There are no longer those juvenile battles and each one comes through strong, vibrant, full of humor and different, full of life and we are awfully lucky. It is right that Bar be there but boy do I miss her . . ."

George's mother and aunt flew to China to spend the holidays with him. He assured the kids on December 2: "All's well here. Take care of your mother at Christmas. If

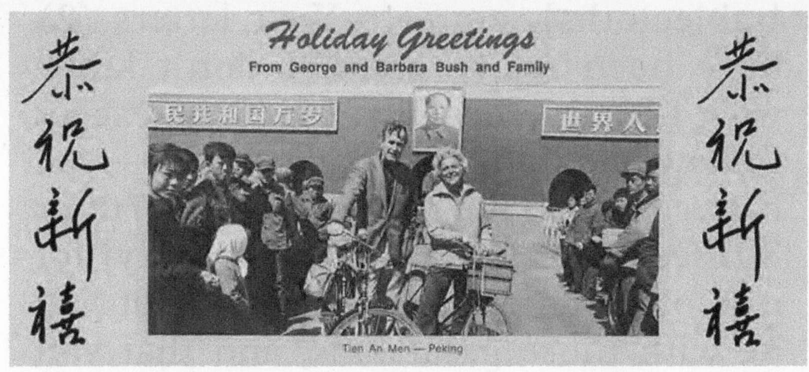

George and Barbara's Christmas card from China.

she seems down once in a while hold out your hand to her. Make her very happy. She gives us all so much all the time."

Then, on December 16, 1974, George wrote to Barbara:

> Dear Bar,
>
> I love you. It's bad being apart except for one thing — I always 'count the ways' when you're gone. Don't get me wrong — I'm not depressed, indeed I'm happy for reasons I'll describe, but I miss you very much . . . Reasons I'm happy — [although] Hawaii was fun and very very interesting I am glad to be home . . . Your great [chests] and other stateside stuff was all here and all most welcome. I miss your leadership in things like frames, [bedspreads], those

[tablecloths], etc. . . . Your letters (2) have been really great. I don't know what I want to be when I grow up except I know one thing for positive sure — you better be with me. January 6th or 7th or 8th seems far away, but that's [okay] for it is of paramount importance that you be with those great kids, and that you hug Paula and that you tell them all including Don that we love them[.] Then when Christmas is gone you can hurry back here . . . They are skating on the lake near the summer palace. So much to say yet I can't say it . . . except tell those wieners I love them and tell their mother she is the great and the most everything in the world, and that she is loved and missed . . . and that each day brings her home (home isn't that funny) sooner . . . I'll write before Christmas but knowing the pouch . . . Merry Christmas from a guy in China who loves you very very much . . . It's just not the same here. I love you.

Poppy

The Bushes had been in China for a year when news arrived from Washington: President Ford wanted George to serve as the new director of the Central Intelligence

Agency. It was a loaded request. In 1975, the C.I.A. was facing major scrutiny from Congress, the press, and the public for abuse of power from obtaining information on citizens to alleged assassination attempts. The agency needed someone to restore public confidence and conduct necessary restructuring.

As George read the White House's proposal, Barbara's eyes filled with tears. The C.I.A. was flooded with scandal, and she had flashbacks to his R.N.C. post of long nights, days apart, and endless attacks. "I remember Camp David," Barbara told George, referring to the time she told George not to take the R.N.C. job, but after meeting with the president at Camp David, George had felt it was his duty to serve. In Beijing, staring at the president's proposition, George's patriotism prevailed again. They were returning to Washington, D.C.

On November 19, 1975, Barbara wrote to the kids back home:

> "17 days have gone by since that fateful Sunday morning here when we got the cable, Pop's eyes only, from the White House, signed by Henry Kissinger . . . He, of course accepted the job, because he has been brought up to think that one

should say yes to tough jobs and should serve at the President's convenience. My Gosh, the C.I.A.!! What a challenge! . . . I can see the adrenaline begin to flow and he is getting eager to get home and tackle this fascinating new job. My initial reaction was one of great sorrow for there is no question in my mind that this is the end of any political dreams that George may have had. And selfishly, I have loved being a part of his life these last few years. The exciting part is that he will do a good job and he will be in on the excitement of foreign policy which is where some of his interests lie."

George's swearing in as director of the C.I.A.

"He cannot share this part of his life with me, but I am thrilled to see that he is so excited."

— BARBARA, WRITING TO HER FAMILY

On January 30, 1976, George replaced C.I.A. Director William Colby. The agency didn't waste any time putting George to work. "George is working longer hours than ever," Barbara wrote to her friends a month after his appointment. She went back to her old clubs and served on boards, but she could not shake a deep void that was developing inside. Years later, she wrote in her memoirs, "I was very depressed, lonely, and unhappy." The children had left the nest and George could not tell her what was happening in the agency; she felt empty and disconnected. "Night after night George held me weeping in his arms while I tried to explain my feelings. I almost wonder why he didn't leave me," she recalled. "Sometimes the pain was so great, I felt the urge to drive into a tree or an oncoming car. When that happened, I would pull over to the side of the road until I felt okay."

George urged her to seek professional help, but Barbara refused to believe she wouldn't be able to shake this off and keep moving forward. For six months, she dragged and did not receive help and only revealed her true feelings to George. "My 'code' told me that you should not think about self, but others. And yet, there I was, wallowing in self-pity. I knew it was wrong, but couldn't seem to pull out of it," she wrote. "I wish I could pinpoint the day it went away, but I can't. All I know is that after about six months it just did. I was so lucky."

When Ford lost the election to Jimmy Carter in November of 1976, George stepped down from the C.I.A. position before the January 1977 inauguration. The Bushes put their Washington house on the market, and Barbara flew to Houston to pick out a new house.

It seemed like they were on their way to a quiet retirement.

Eighteen:
Back in the Races

"George Bush is running for president."

— BARBARA, IN HER DIARY ON
SEPTEMBER 18, 1978

George Bush has actively been running for president since January of this year. He has done all those things that he should have done in order to get the Republican nomination. He has been campaigning and doing fundraisers for republican candidates all around the U.S.A. He has carefully avoided working in contested republican primary races. He is trying to get in touch with key people — key to nominating the G.O.P. candidate in 1980. It suddenly occurred to me today that I should be keeping a diary, so I am going to try, I am going to try to keep a diary of my role, my part. If it's only staying home. At this moment in the campaign I am doing little. I am speaking pretty often on China, showing slides. I am doing a little traveling with George. I wish I could do more. I have such respect for his drive and energy. He goes day after day — flying, speaking, on and on.

George began to campaign quietly in 1978. His greatest competitor for the Republican nomination was Governor Ronald Reagan of California — a former actor who had the strong name recognition that George needed, so George and Barbara raced around the country.

While flying from Mexico to Houston on March 1, 1979, she wrote to a friend:

"George and I are traveling just all the time. I do not get to go with him as much as I would like for I have a pretty full schedule of my own. Just to give you a little idea of our life we left town on Tuesday, Feb 20th for Atlanta, George, Feb 21st flew to San Diego, Cal. Feb 22nd flew from desert to Florida — Pensacola, Feb 23rd — Tallahassee, Feb 24th — Fort Walton, Feb 25th — Vero Beach, Feb 26th — Hobe [Sound], Feb 27 — Boca Raton, Ft. Pierce, and Ft. Lauderdale, Feb 28th flew to Acapulco, Mexico for YPO Meeting (Young Presidents Organization) . . .

George spoke to all 1200 and I had a nicely attended class. (He spoke on foreign affairs and I on China.) We flew off to Mexico City today and had breakfast with some Mexican friends and are now finally going home. 9 days away and 8 different beds! Oh, I will be glad to get home!"

After George left the C.I.A., he and Barbara moved from Palisade Lane to a new home in Houston. Their children were spread out around the country, except for Jeb and Columba, who brought the first two of many grandchildren to the Bush family, George and Noelle. Jeb worked on the 1980 campaign for his father and took a leave of absence from Texas Commerce Bank to help. Over in his hometown of Midland, George W. had fallen in love with a girl named Laura Welch. They were introduced by mutual friends in July 1977 and they were married by November 1977. In 1978, George W. ran for congress and lost. (He would run a successful campaign for governor in 1995 and serve until 2000.) Neil had helped George on his campaign and was working on obtaining his master's degree at Tulane University. He had also met Sharon Smith, who he would marry in the summer of 1980. Marvin was enrolled at the University of Virginia and Doro was starting her freshman year at Boston College.

> "One very good thing came out of that campaign. The children treated me like an adult for the first time. Before that, they asked me all the 'peanut butter and jelly' questions and George all the 'steak and potato' questions. Then they discovered I could campaign with the best of them. My thinking about them changed also. They no longer were children. They were able, bright, loving, loyal young men and women."
>
> — BARBARA BUSH

By January 1980, George was looking like a contender for the Republican nomination. "George Bush was once thought to be a political lightweight, little more than a perennial Vice-Presidential possibility. That estimate was dramatically refuted by his startling upset of Ronald Reagan in the Iowa precinct caucuses on Jan. 21," wrote Roy Reed for the *New York Times* on February 10, 1980.

Reed compared the two contenders in his article: "In one corner was the aging former Governor of California, papered over in suit and tie, who will be almost 70 years old at the next Presidential inauguration. In the other corner," Reed continued. "was the challenger: lean, hard and athletic, 6 feet 2 inches tall, 190 pounds, a three-mile-a-day runner, all-American healthy, fit and youthful. Mr. Bush will be a boy of 56 when the next President is sworn in."

During the campaign, George traveled extensively. "I saw Barbara twice this week: once in the middle of the night at Des Moines, Iowa, and once briefly in Indianapolis," George dictated to his campaign diary in 1979. "She's worked hard and getting good press."

Barbara had an enormous role in the campaign. While they tried to travel together as much as possible, they were able to cover more ground when they split up. In the beginning, she was uncomfortable speaking in front of crowds and she would lean on her China slideshow to facilitate conversations, but toward the end of the campaigning, she was accepting interviews on George's behalf. Nancy Cain of *The Macomb Daily* wrote on September 20, 1980: "Barbara Bush is no ordinary grandmother . . . Wedged between her family life and personal projects, she is on the campaign trail six days a week, with all the banquets, speeches and handshaking ap-

George and Barbara with their kids after winning the election.

pearances that accompany politics. 'I've been very lucky,' the snow-haired, immaculately groomed woman said with a smile. 'I really like meeting people, traveling. I'm learning all the time. I'm happy.' "

Happy happy 54th
Love you — I love you very much. Nothing — campaign separations, people, nothing will ever change that — I can't ever really tell you how much I love you.

Your 55 yr. old husband,
Pop

At the end of May 1980, George decided to withdraw from the presidential race. "It was a tough decision but when we realized that George couldn't win the nomination but could win [New Jersey] and Ohio and all that would do would be to make it harder for the Republicans to win in the fall then

George and Barbara at a campaign event.

we realized we must pull out," Barbara wrote in her diary in the summer of 1980.

At the Republican Convention in Detroit, Michigan, in July 1980, George gave a speech urging supporters to get behind the Reagan campaign. Hope in the vice presidency had been lost; former President Ford was the frontrunner. Back in the hotel, Jeb moped as Barbara packed, and George reminded them: "We came to this convention to leave politics with style and we are going to do it." Then the phone rang at 11:30 p.m., it was Ronald Reagan. Due to fundamental disagreements on how the chain of command would work between a former president and serving president, the Reagan-Ford ticket was tossed. The former governor of California wanted George. With the hotel phone pressed to his ear George told Reagan, he'd be honored.

"There was never a hint of negative feeling left over from our fight for the presidential nomination because Reagan's instinct, I learned, is to think the best of the people he works with. It was clear that once he made his decision on the vice presidency, he viewed the Reagan-Bush ticket not simply as a convenient political alliance but as a partnership. We would run and serve together as a team."

— GEORGE BUSH

President Reagan and Vice President Bush were sworn into office on January 20, 1981. Barbara held the family Bible where George placed his left hand and raised his right as U.S. Supreme Court Justice Potter Stewart conducted the ceremony.

After the festivities quieted, George and Barbara pulled up to their new home, Number One Observatory Circle, a white Queen Anne–style house studded with olive

George giving a speech during a campaign event.

President Ronald Reagan and First Lady Nancy Reagan with Vice President George Bush and Barbara Bush.

George and Barbara as V.P. and Second Lady.

green shutters. Inside, the staff had unpacked their bags and prepared dinner — they were expecting over 150 relatives. The event would be the first of 1,192 held at their house during their eight vice presidential years. Later that evening, George and Barbara gazed out their bedroom window. Through January's bare trees was a view of the glowing Capitol and Washington Monument.

Number One Observatory Circle has been the home of the second family since 1974. The first keepers were Vice President Nelson Rockefeller and his wife, Happy. Vice President Walter Mondale and his wife, Joan, were the first to live in the house. George and Barbara took it over from the Mondales. With the help of professional decorators, Barbara turned the residence into a home that felt warm and comfortable while honoring its stately character. "We're using it as a home instead of a museum," she told reporters on a tour.

Between 1981 and 1989, George and Barbara spent more time outside of Washington than they did in it. (Despite the thousands of events they hosted and attended at the White House.) They visited all fifty states and sixty-five foreign countries during those eight years. "George and I traveled an

Barbara shows off the sign for their new home.

estimated 1.3 million miles, which is about fifty-four times around the world," recalled Barbara.

One job requirement of the vice president was to attend the funerals of foreign dignitaries. He attended so many that family friend and campaign manager James Baker came up with the slogan for the V.P. — You die, I'll fly. George used the ceremonies as opportunities to meet the incoming leadership. In one such instance, when Soviet head of state Konstantin Chernenko died, George met Mikhail Gorbachev in Moscow — a relationship that would be critical in his presidential years.

During his vice presidency, George served on several task forces, including the Presidential Task Force for Regulatory Relief, which reviewed pending and past government regulations on businesses. He was selected by Reagan to lead the National Security Crisis Management Group. He traveled on behalf of the administration for diplomacy, such as his visit to Europe in 1983 to discuss arms control.

He also became well known for his loyalty to the president. The famous incident occurred just months after the inauguration. It was March 30, 1981, and George was on a twelve-hour round-trip to Texas, stopping in Fort Worth and Austin for three speeches and one meeting. As his plane was taxiing in Austin, George received the news: President Reagan had been shot. The vice president needed to return to Washington. While they flew east, information trickled in — the president was in surgery and expected to recover, and finally he was out of surgery and stable.

The plan was for George to land at Joint

Base Andrews in Maryland, then take the Marine helicopter to the White House — in time for the evening news and to quickly send a message to the country and the world that the U.S. government was operating. However, George had another idea — although the White House landing would have shaved ten minutes off his arrival time, he wanted to land at One Observatory Circle, as is routine for the V.P., and drive to the White House. His explanation to his *Air Force II* team: "Only the president lands on the South Lawn."

While on the flight back to Washington,

George with President Reagan in the Oval Office.

George called Barbara. "I really needed to hear his voice, and he must have sensed that," she remembered. When the helicopter landed at their house, she met him on the pad. "He gave me a hug and then left with Ed [Meese] for the fifteen-minute drive to the White House."

Barbara was content in her role as second lady. "Those stories about how ghastly it is to be married to a political figure. You have a choice," she told reporter Gloria Borger for *Savvy* in August 1983. "You can do something and share things with your husband, or you can stay home, which would be dumb. When you have the opportunity that I have to do something that makes a difference, you're lucky and you ought to do it."

Barbara used her influence to raise funds for national literacy programs. In 1984, she published *C. Fred's Story,* about the family cocker spaniel and his daily adventures as the vice president's pup. The book raised $100,000 for Literacy Volunteers of America and Laubach Literacy Action, two organizations that were actively combating illiteracy.

"She is totally engrossed in working for literacy programs. She cares about people. She really cares. She has her own identity, which politics could not ask for her to surrender. She is supportive, but that doesn't mean she refuses to speak up," George wrote to *Savvy* in August 1983. "She cheers for me and I cheer for her. When she hurts, it hurts me too. When I hurt, she holds out her arms. It's been like that for thirty-eight years."

On January 6, 1986, George and Barbara were on their way to an NBC dinner. Just before they left Marvin called to say the Swedish ambassador's wife had left her stole at the house. *Could they please drop it off on their way?* "George said that was easy as we were dining right across the street," she jotted into her diary. When they pulled up to the embassy — police escort and all — Barbara pressed the doorbell with the forgotten stole in hand, and when the door opened there were her kids, friends, and family members — "It was a 41st wedding anniversary surprise party!" Barbara wrote in her diary.

A year later, George wrote to Barbara:

> "Let's see Bar — 42 years ago this minute I was a nervous wreck — you, too, maybe. Anyway, here we are 42 years later, and I am a very happy guy — the luckiest in the world actually. I have a skinny, miles walking wife; I have

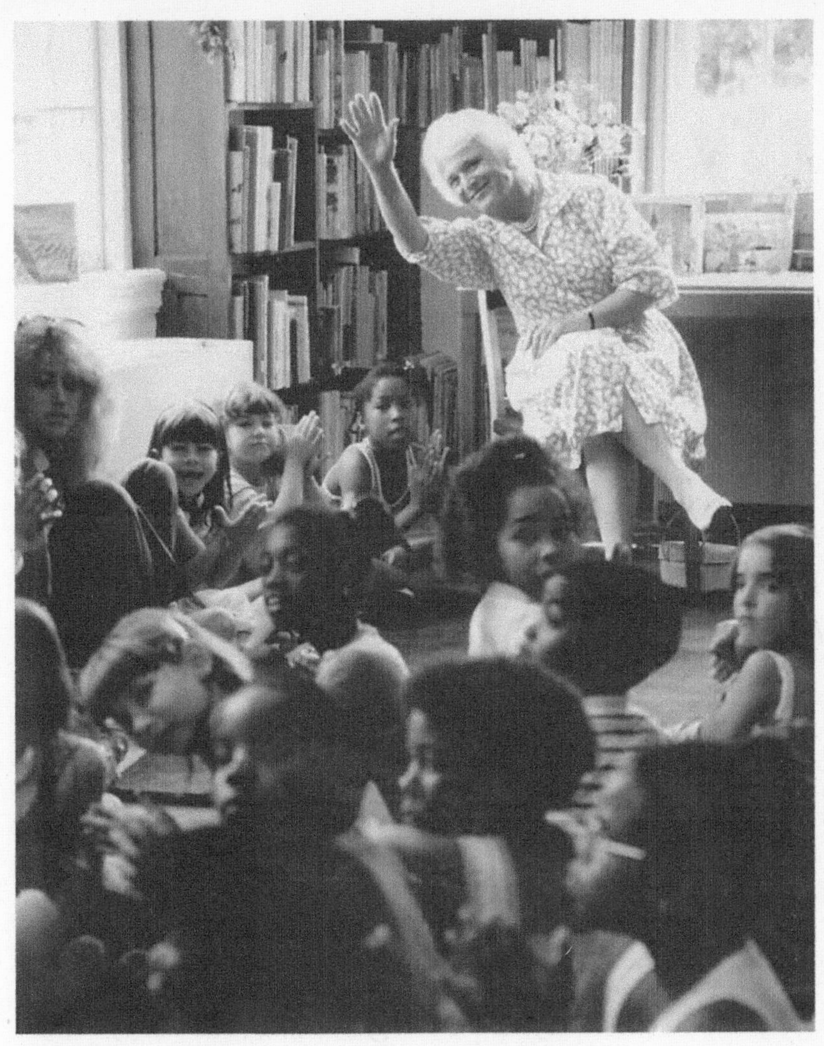

Barbara reading to group of students.

a lot of grandkids (so do you) and they all, each and everyone, bring me happiness just thinking about them. Our own kids are great; our dog is in tough shape, but he's given us joy; our house wasn't

Barbara speaking about C. Fred's Story.

even nicked by the seas or the snow; we aren't rich, but we are awful lucky. We don't owe any money and if either of us gets sick the other guy can pay the bills. We have a lot of friends — no real enemies [though] there are some who aren't exactly rooting hard for us; we have quiet faith that gives us strength; so — when we count our blessings we've got to count on a long long time. How do I love you? Let me count the ways — one, er, ah lets' see — I'm not good at that. But I love you very much. Have for more than 42 years and will for the next [however] many lie ahead. I can't ever say it too well, but you know that, don't ya?

Love,
Pop

Barbara and George.

George and Barbara in bed with grandkids.

Over the course of their eight years in Washington, the Bush family had grown to include ten grandchildren. The little ones grew up running around the lawn of Number One Observatory Circle, seeing their grandfather take off in the Marine helicopter, and walking in the middle of Secret Service details. Their naivety won the hearts of Americans when many of them became part of the campaign from 1987 to 1988. In their little worlds, their grandparents were normal: they read to them, let them crawl into their bed in the morning, disciplined them, and were always there for a hug.

George started to think about campaigning early into Reagan's second term. He assembled a team — Lee Atwater and Roger Ailes. But there was a darkness to the 1988 election year: The campaigning on both sides was harsh and negative. Rumors of affairs spread about George. "Of course it wasn't true," recalled Doro Bush Koch. "It was one more example of how people who run for office become public property, and how some people in the media will stop at nothing to bring them down."

They campaigned tirelessly. When Michael Dukakis and his team took a double redeye and flew coast to coast on the eve of the election, Barbara took control. "Bush's handlers argued for a similar marathon. But

The growing family on the lawn at Walker's Point.

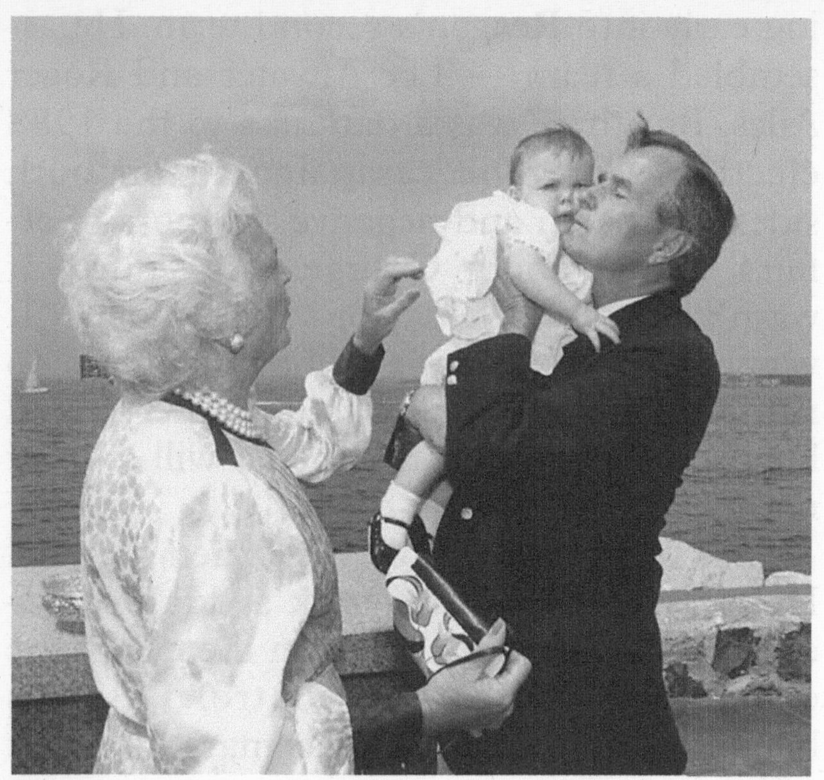

George holding baby Ellie.

Barbara put her foot down. 'People are going to vote the way they're going to vote,' she said. 'We're going to Texas.' "

On November 8, 1988, George and Barbara voted early in the morning, spent some time at their friend's house in Houston, and then went over to the Houstonian Hotel. After a few early reports of victory, the results were in — George had received 53 percent of the popular vote and 426 electoral votes. He would be the next president of the United States. "I still find it incredible and almost impossible to believe," he told his daughter Doro years later.

George was sixty-four years old and Barbara was sixty-three. He had served his country as a Navy pilot, congressman, ambassador to the United Nations, U.S. liaison to the People's Republic of China, director of Central Intelligence, and vice president.

The next morning Barbara wrote in her diary: "I awakened this morning with the President-elect of the United States of America."

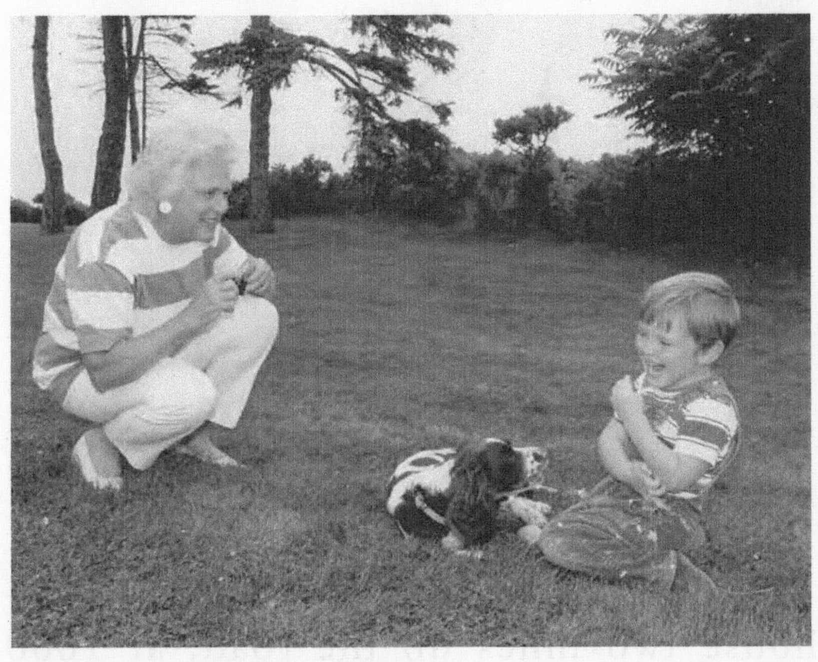

Barbara and Sam in Maine.

George campaigning in Jackson Hole, Wyoming.

Barbara campaigning.

The Bushes were ready for their next house two miles up the road, at 1600 Pennsylvania Avenue.

After Ronald Reagan announced that Gampy would be his running mate, my grandparents had coffee with him and Nancy Reagan. After months of hard campaigning against one another, they were coming together. Many people know that my grandmother has a way with words, but that morning, she truly made an impact on United States history. Just as they were wrapping up, she left Ronald and Nancy with a promising confirmation: "You're not going to be sorry. We're going to work our tails off for you," she said with confidence.

Biographer Jon Meacham, author of *Destiny and Power: The American Odyssey of George Herbert Walker Bush* and a close friend of the family, believes that without my grandmother, my grandfather would not have been president. This was due to many reasons, but one was her choice of words that morning. "Having her say that and having your grandfather embody that convinced Reagan that Bush could be trusted," said Meacham. "Your grandfather would not have been president and your uncle would not have been president if he had not been Reagan's vice president. That's just not arguable."

If you ask Ganny, she'll laugh it off and deny any influence.

NINETEEN: FIRST COUPLE

"Some see leadership as high drama and the sound of trumpets calling, and sometimes it is that. But I see history as a book with many pages, and each day we fill a page with acts of hopefulness and meaning. The new breeze blows, a page turns, the story unfolds. And so, today a chapter begins, a small and stately story of unity, diversity, and generosity — shared, and written, together."

— PRESIDENT GEORGE H. W. BUSH,
FROM HIS INAUGURAL ADDRESS,
JANUARY 20, 1989

President Bush was sworn in on the bicentennial of George Washington's inauguration. He placed his hand on the Bible that George Washington had touched during his inauguration two hundred years before in 1789. In a teal coat that slightly revealed her white pearls that matched her snowy hair, Barbara held the Bible firmly and stared with determined loyalty at her husband.

George honored President Ronald Reagan at the very beginning of the ceremony by saying, "Thank you for the great things that you have done for our country," which resulted in a standing ovation. He went on: "No president, no government can teach us to remember what is best in what we are. But if the man you have chosen to lead this government can help make a difference; if he can celebrate the quieter, deeper successes that are made not of gold and silk but of better hearts and finer souls; if he can do these things, then he must."

After the ceremony, the Sergeant at Arms of the House, said, "Mr. President."

George stood there quietly waiting for President Reagan. He was not used to his new title. "I feel something that is between an affectionate hug and a kidney punch — the Silver Fox telling me to get going," he laughs before the House of Representatives luncheon on the day of the inauguration.

Barbara had earned the Silver Fox nickname from her children, but *Time* ran with it on the cover on January 21, 1989: "The

Barbara looks on as George is sworn in as the forty-first president of the United States.

Silver Fox: Barbara Bush brings a refreshing new style to the White House." Inside she's lauded for her candor and honesty, which was seen as a welcome transition after the previous administration: "After eight years of new-money flash and glitz, of appearances over substance, of friends over family, Barbara Bush's unspoken message may be as important as anything she may do: there is honor in motherhood; it is O.K. to be a size 14; a lined face is the price of living; and growing old is nothing to get frantic about."

As First Lady, she continued her literacy efforts, launching the Barbara Bush Foundation for Family Literacy in the first few months. Barbara Bush's *Story Time* aired throughout the presidency on ABC Radio. She read children's books aloud and had special guests like Big Bird and Bugs Bunny. *Each day we should do something to help others,* said Barbara and she set out to meet that goal contributing to many charities, including the National Committee for Prevention of Child Abuse, the Leukemia Society of America, the Ronald McDonald House, Eugene Lang's "I Have a Dream" Foundation, Boys and Girls Clubs across the United States, United Way, and more.

Working together to make a difference.

"We get enormous strength from our family. Not just our children and grandchildren, but our brothers and sisters. It's always been like that. And more so now. Once you're in a position where you're really isolated from people, you count more heavily on your children and your closest friends."

— BARBARA BUSH

The White House intentionally became a home for the First Family — right down to the grandkids sliding across the floor in their socks before slipping into a hiding spot. Christmas was a spectacle of white lights and fake snow frosting the trees; it took months to plan, days to execute, and many volunteers. Christmas mornings they awoke at Camp David. When the grandkids were there it was noisy and playful, but the surrounding walking paths provided a quiet solitude unavailable in downtown Washington, D.C.

The Bushes opened the White House to 40,000 people annually, and hosted twenty-nine state dinners in honor of foreign leaders such as Queen Elizabeth and the Duke of Edinburgh of Great Britain, King Hassan of Morocco, and Prime Minister Mazowiecki of Poland. The administration hosted

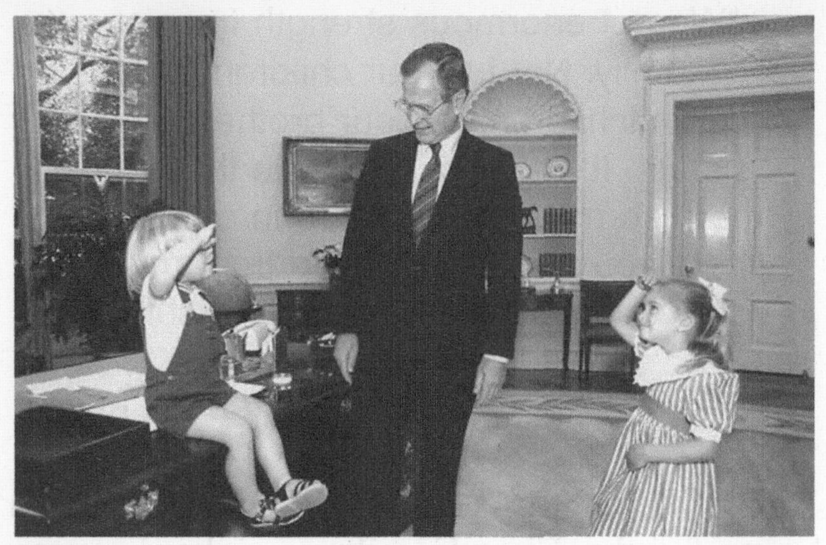

Pierce and Lauren in the Oval Office.

about two foreign lunches a month — sometimes George would dine with the prime minister while Barbara might have lunch with the wife in another room. Each year, they hosted a congressional barbecue, feeding over 800 guests with picnic tables and loud, live country music. The Bushes also hosted a variety of informal gatherings. When there was a rare gap on both their schedules, they arranged movie nights. If the weather cooperated, they would have a buffet in the First Lady's garden before retreating inside for popcorn and soda.

The many events were also part of George's personal diplomacy. With varied posts, his Rolodex of foreign contacts was thick, but he became known for calling diplomats to check in, see how they were doing, and hear what struggles they were facing. He was establishing personal connections in case he had to ask for a favor down the road.

Ask he did, most notably during the Gulf War. Saddam Hussein invaded Kuwait on August 2, 1990. Hussein occupied Kuwait in a dictatorial fashion. The United Nations placed economic sanctions on Iraq, but those along with a naval blockade weren't enough for Hussein to withdraw. The United States assembled the largest coalition since World War II with forces and

Marshall biking into the Oval Office.

contributions from thirty-four countries. Operation Desert Storm began on January 16, 1991, and ended on February 28, 1991. "Kuwait is liberated. Iraq's army is defeated. Our military objectives are met," said George.

Before the war broke out, Barbara could see that George could not think about anything else. He worried about sending troops and about not acting. Barbara called two of George's closest friends, Spike Hemingway and Arnold Schwarzenegger, and invited them to Camp David.

The kids and grandkids filled the house, too, but George's mind was elsewhere. After the kids left, he sat down to write a letter:

> Dear George, Jeb, Neil, Marvin, Doro,
> . . . First, I can't begin to tell you how great it was to have you here at Camp David . . . I hope I didn't seem moody. I tried not to.
>
> When I came into this job I vowed that I would never ring my hands and talk about the 'loneliest job in the world' or ring my hands about the 'pressures of the trials.'
>
> Having said that I <u>have</u> been concerned about what lies ahead. There is no

'loneliness' though because I am backed by a first rate team of knowledgeable and

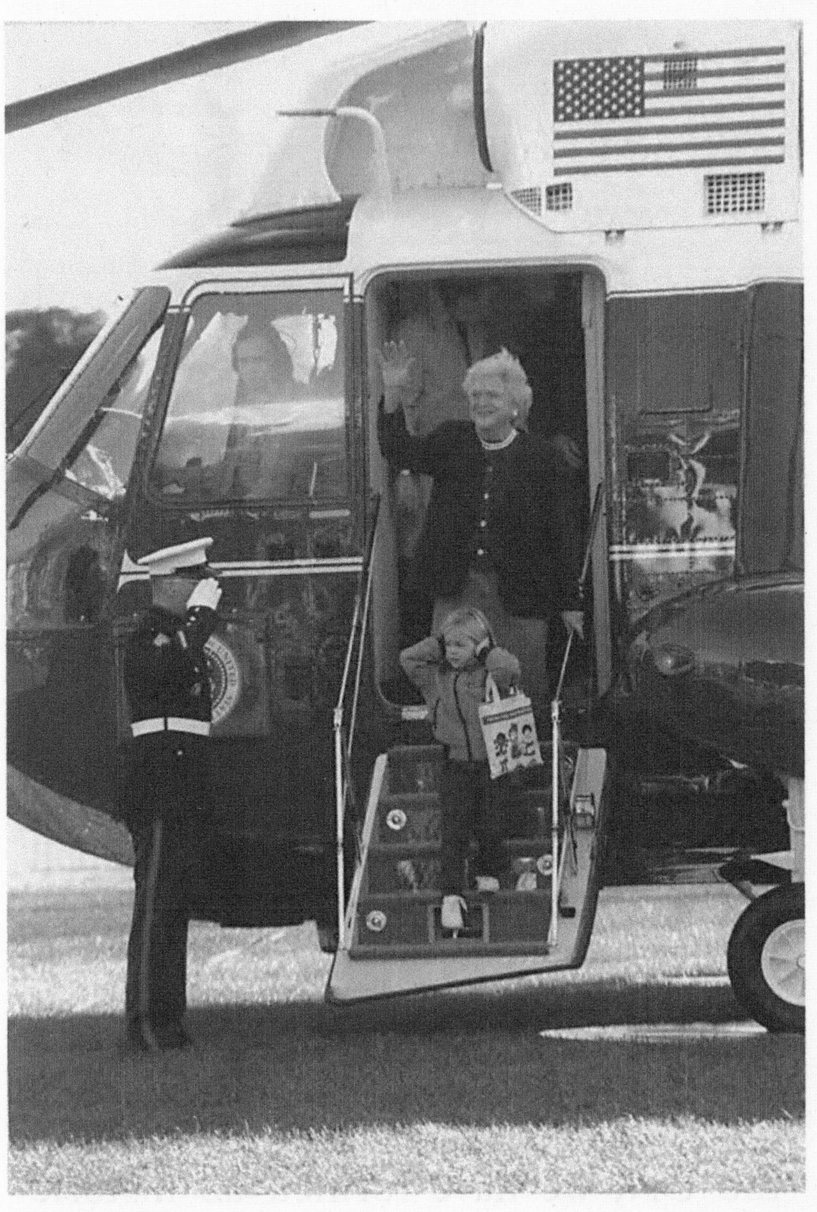

Marshall covering her ears as she exits Marine One.

George with puppies on White House lawn.

committed people. No President had been more blessed in this regard.

I have thought long and hard about what might have to be done. As I write this letter at year's end, there is still some hope that Iraq's dictator will pull out of Kuwait. I vary on this. Sometimes I think he might, at others I think he is too unrealistic — too ignorant of what he might face. I have the peace of mind that comes from knowing that we have tried hard for peace. We have gone to the UN; we have formed an historic coalition; there have been diplomatic initiatives from country after country.

And here we are scant 16 days from a very important date — the date set by the UN for his total compliance with all UN resolutions including getting out of Kuwait — totally.

I guess what I want you to know as a father is this: Every Human life is precious. When the question is asked 'How many lives are you willing to sacrifice?' [it] tears at my heart. The answer of course, is none — none at all. We have waited to give sanctions a chance, we have moved a tremendous force so as to reduce the risk to every American soldier if force has to be used; but the question of loss of life still lingers and plagues the heart . . . I know my stance must cause you a little grief from time to time and this hurts me; but here at 'years-end' I just wanted you to know that I feel:

— every human life is precious — the little Iraqi kids' too.

— Principle must be adhered to — Saddam cannot profit in any way at all from his aggression and from his brutalizing the people of Kuwait.

— and sometimes in life you have to act as you think best — you can't compromise, you can't give in — even if your critics are loud and numerous.

So, dear kids — batten down the hatches . . .

Devotedly,
Dad

Over the course of his presidency, his personal relationships helped to facilitate the destruction of the Berlin Wall and bring a unified Germany into the world. George developed a respectful relationship with Mikhail Gorbachev, leader of the Soviet Union, who was reluctant that German reunification would make them seem weak. George and Gorbachev agreed the citizens

George seems overwhelmed by balloons on his birthday.

should decide, and they voted for unification.

When the wall came down on October 3, 1990, George called German Chancellor Helmut Kohl from the Oval Office to congratulate him, and Kohl thanked George.

Raisa Gorbachev accompanied Barbara on her famous commencement speech at Wellesley College. Before her arrival, students were protesting the school's selection. Barbara wrote: "According to them: 'Barbara Bush has gained recognition through the achievements of her husband,' Wellesley, they said, 'teaches us that we will be rewarded on the basis of our own merit, not on that of a spouse.' " Some back and forth resulted between Barbara and a few students, and it was ultimately decided that she would come. When Barbara and Raisa delivered the speech on June 1, 1990, she seemed to have won the students over who received them with a loud applause. "Whether you are talking about education, career, or service, you are talking about life . . . and life must have joy. It's supposed to be fun! One of the reasons I made the most important decision of my life . . . to marry George Bush . . . is because he made me laugh. It's true, sometimes we've laughed through our tears . . . but that shared laughter has been one of our strongest bonds." Her final sign off though did the trick: "And who knows? Somewhere out in this audience may even be someone who will one day follow in my footsteps, and preside over the White House as the President's spouse. I wish him well!"

In 1990, George signed the Clean Air Act, which curbed four major health hazards: acid rain, urban air pollution, toxic air emissions, and stratospheric ozone depletion; and the American Disabilities Act, which prohibits discrimination against citizens with disabilities.

Promises made during the 1988 campaign were broken when George raised taxes to account for a growing deficit. "This is the first time in my Presidency that I've made an appeal like this to you, the American people. With your help, we can at last put this budget crisis behind us and face the challenges that lie ahead," he told the public, but the decision resulted in a loss of confidence and declining approval ratings of the president. "Read my lips . . . I lied!" read the cover of the *New York Post*.

As the 1992 election approached, unemployment rates were still high in parts of the country, and George was seen as not offer-

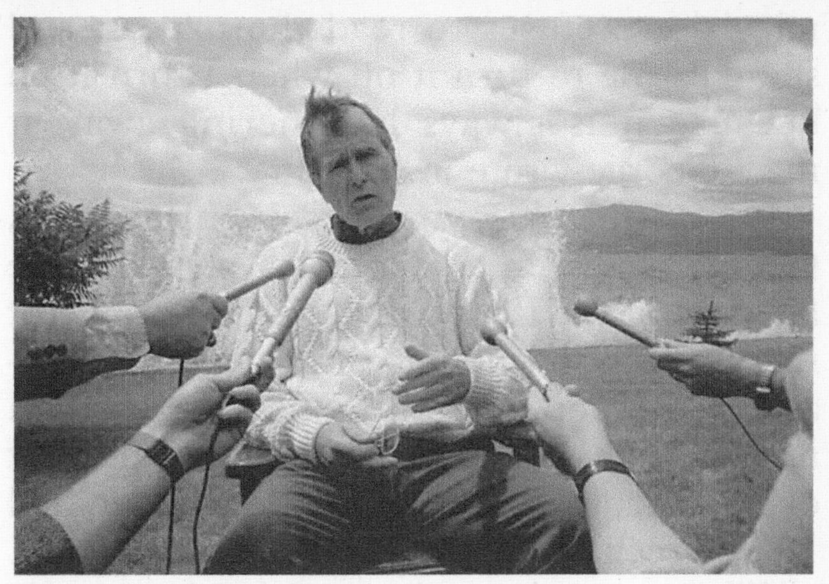

George with the media.

ing a comprehensive solution to that problem. "As President Bush travels the country in search of re-election, he seems unable to escape a central problem: This career politician, who has lived the cloistered life of a top Washington bureaucrat for decades, is having trouble presenting himself to the electorate as a man in touch with middle-class life," wrote Andrew Rosenthal for the *New York Times* on Wednesday, February 5, 1992.

"This is all extraordinarily tough on Barbara. She is still wildly popular and gets a wonderful response, but I can tell she is hurting for me. She refuses to watch the television; refuses to read the papers; and she tells me to turn it off when I turn it on because it is always hammering away at me," George wrote in his diary.

Also, since his vice presidential days, George was seen as drifting away from the far right of the Republican Party. Ross Perot ran as an independent capturing a percentage of the popular vote. When the election results came in, Bill Clinton had 43 percent of the vote; Ross Perot, an independent, had 18.9 percent; and George had 37.5 percent.

"We respect the majesty of the democratic system," said George at the Westin Galleria Hotel in Houston, Texas. "There is important work to be done and America must always come first."

He went on: "I want to thank my entire family with a special emphasis on my wife Barbara. She has inspired this entire nation and I think the country will always be grateful."

He waved to everyone with one hand and then reached for Barbara with the other before they exited the stage.

Visiting Ganny and Gampy at the White House

When I was two years old, my mom, brother, and I moved from Portland, Maine, to Washington, D.C. My parents had recently separated and my mom needed the support of her parents who happened to live in the White House.

We visited all the time — had sleepovers, stayed over for weekends. Sometimes my mom would drop us off when she had a date. As five- and seven-year-olds, free rein (for the most part) at the White House was a dream. We spent our days running through the large corridors and playing hide and seek through the state parlors and generally wreaking a bit of havoc, I'm sure. Hide and seek was especially a blast. With 132 rooms, 35 bathrooms, 412 doors, 28 fireplaces, and 8 stairwells — there was no shortage of hiding places. Looking back, I'm sure the staff was overwhelmed.

There were many friendly White House ushers but our favorite was Ramsey. Every time we saw him, Ramsey would hold out two closed fists — "pick a hand." We'd pick a hand and he'd open it and reveal a piece of candy or a quarter. We thought it was the greatest thing in the world. Now that I think of it, we somehow always picked the right hand.

Sam and I, along with our other cousins who lived nearby, had the special privilege of being Christmas Elves during the White House Christmas festivities. We took our responsibilities very seriously, one of which was helping to clean up the White House once the holiday season came to a close. We'd put on our elf costumes and help take down the Christmas ornaments, unwrap the lights from the trees and sweep the endless piles of fake snow. Being the good girl that I was, I would follow directions and use the broom to sweep the snow into the trash bins. Sam, being the naughty boy that he was, would take the trash bins that I had spent so much time filling and pour them out on my head.

I loved going to visit my grandfather in the Oval Office. I had zero clue that he had an important job or that living in the White House wasn't normal. I would hang out on the Oval Office floor while he held important meetings — foreign leaders, cabinet members, and the like. I sat there with my toys or riding my tricycle around the room, oblivious to what was going on. One time, Gampy had a meeting with a foreign diplomat. I needed to use the bathroom so I

Grandkids Ellie, Marshall, and Sam dressed as elves in front of the White House Christmas tree.

tapped Gampy on the shoulder — "um excuse me Gampy, can I use the bathroom?" With a confused look, he tells me that of course I can, I know where it is. Thirty seconds later, another tap on his shoulder. "Um, excuse me, Gampy, but did you leave that poo poo in the toilet?" I don't think he ever lived that one down.

I loved spending time in the White House with my grandparents. Though I didn't fully understand the true specialness of it then, I look back now with the fondest memories.

Twenty: FLFW & FFLFW

George and Barbara went from occupying the highest office to waking up on January 21, 1992, as Former Leader of the Free World and Former First Lady of the Free World, 1,400 miles from Washington in Houston, Texas.

The day before, they woke up in the White House for the last time — calling for coffee, reading the news, and conducting their typical morning rituals with added emotion. They walked with the dogs along the South Grounds before welcoming the Clintons. "Then came the moment when the mantle was lifted from the back of my superb husband and placed on Bill Clinton's," remembered Barbara.

Humble in victory, gracious in defeat, went the mantra in the Bush home, and George and Barbara held their heads high as best they could. "Barbara is wonderful,"

George told his diary on the last day of his presidency.

> She's strong and what a First Lady she's been — popular and wonderful. And suddenly she is eclipsed by the new wave, the lawyer, the wife with an office in the White House; but time will tell and history will show that she was beloved because she was real and she cared and she gave [all] of herself. She has been fantastic in every way, and my, how the people around here love her, and my, how that staff rejoices in the fact that she came their way. But we'll make it in Houston — I know we will. We kid about her cooking. We kid about no staff, no valets, no shined shoes and no pressed suits. We did that before and we can do it again. It's my last day as President of the United States.

George and Barbara flew out of Washington, D.C., to Houston, Texas, for the last time on *Air Force One.* "It hurts," George admitted. Just over 60 percent of the country voted against him. He felt he had let many people down, especially his supporters and staff, and he had a difficult time moving forward, but Barbara wasn't going to let him retreat.

She got to work quickly setting into motion plans for the vacant lot they owned. George and Barbara purchased the lot over a decade earlier and had planned to build a Houston home until George was elected vice president. Now was the time to build. "You know, I'm not one who looks back. I just say how lucky I was to have been there," said Barbara when asked about that period in time. "We loved the people [in the White House], so that was very difficult, but when we got home it was unbelievable the crowds that greeted us and there were people with trucks saying welcome home George and Barbara."

They weren't sitting in the Oval Office, but they were still busy as ever. At one point after his presidency, George was receiving 100 to 200 pieces of mail a day. Since 1993, the Office of George Bush sent an estimated 149,700 congratulatory letters to Eagle Scouts; 200 to 300 military retirement letters a month; and an estimated 43,500 congratulatory letters have been sent to mark special occasions: births, weddings, birthdays, and anniversaries.

George and Barbara have helped raise $670 million for key projects and causes. Barbara continued to run the Barbara Bush Foundation for Family Literacy, which she

Bar and Poppy.

established while in the White House. She and George have raised nearly $100 million for literacy programs.

"I have spoken of a Thousand Points of Light, of all the community organizations that are spread like stars throughout the Nation, doing good. We will work hand in hand, encouraging, sometimes leading, sometimes being led, rewarding. We will work on this in the White House, in the Cabinet agencies. The old ideas are new again because they're not old, they are timeless: duty, sacrifice, commitment, and a patriotism that finds its expression in taking part and pitching in."

— GEORGE BUSH, FROM HIS 1989 INAUGURAL ADDRESS

While he was president, George started the Points of Light Foundation, which connects individuals interested in volunteering to nonprofits in need of help. About five million individuals volunteer through Points of Light affiliates over the course of a year.

In memory of Robin, George and Barbara became supporters of University of Texas's M.D. Anderson Cancer Center in Houston. They have organized, hosted, and attended events to raise nearly $90 million for cancer research. In 1997, the George Bush School of Government and Public Service, a master's program at Texas A&M University, was established. Since then, he has been an annual lecturer in a number of classes, sits in on special reports and presentations, and still meets with the students before graduation day.

After the 2005 tsunami, George formed an unusual partnership and friendship with former president Bill Clinton. Together they met with leaders and storm victims in Indonesia, Thailand, Sri Lanka, and the

Maldives. The presidents raised close to $100 million and then worked with the American embassies in each of the countries to see that the money was used to help build hospitals, schools, and housing; replace fishing boats; and provide scholarship money. That team would work together again after Hurricane Katrina, Hurricane Ike, and Hurricane Harvey.

In 1995, George W. was elected governor of Texas, and in 1999 Jeb became the governor of Florida. In 2001, George W. was elected as the forty-third president of the United States, marking the second time in the history of the country for a son to assume the presidency after his father (John Adams and John Quincy Adams were the first).

For: Barbara Pierce
January 6, 1994
From: GHWB

Will you marry me? Oops, I forgot, you did that 49 years ago today! I was very happy on that day in 1945 but I am even happier today. You have given me joy that few men know. You have made our boys into men by bawling them out and then, right away, by loving them. You have helped Doro be the sweetest greatest daughter in the whole wide world. I have climbed perhaps the highest mountain in the world, but even that can not hold a candle to being Barbara's husband. Mum used to tell me: "Now George, don't walk ahead." Little did she know I was only trying to keep up — keep up with Barbara Pierce from Onondaga Street in Rye New York. I love you!

After half a century in public service, George began to bounce back to "normal" life. He had loved the ride, and had in fact climbed the tallest mountain, but all around him, he was beginning to realize that politics wasn't the only thing in his life. In his concession speech in 1992, George had told the country, he had planned "to get very active in the grandchild business." In the summers, the driveways of Walker's Point were full of grandkids on bikes. They pitched tents in the yard, served lots of hamburgers and hot dogs, played games, watched movies, tried to find out who left the freezer open and caused all the ice cream to melt . . . typical grandparents stuff.

George and Barbara were happiest when the beds at Walker's Point were full. That also meant more mouths to feed and more laundry to fold, so Barbara taped a note to the backs of the bedroom doors to remind her kids and grandkids of their manners:

BUSH CHILDREN
and GRANDCHILDREN

1. Please hang up damp towels and use twice if possible.
2. Try to make beds and keep room picked up — makes dusting and vacuuming easier.
3. Please collect your gear from around the house and keep in your room.
4. If possible, let the kitchen know your meal plans:
   —picnics
   —specific requests for you or your children
   —missing a meal
5. Breakfast is served from 8 to 9 a.m. — coffee beginning at 6:30 a.m.
6. Please put dirty clothes outside your door every night.
7. Ask Paula what you can do to help her.
8. Above all — have a great time! This is our happiest time of the year!

As they aged, George began to reflect on his life and express his love (and occasional frustration) for his kids and grandkids. He wrote on September 23, 1998:

> Dear Kids,
> Last year there was only a tiny sense of time left — of sand running through the glass. This year, I must confess, I am more aware of that. No fear, no apprehension, just a feeling like 'let's go — there's so much to do and there might not be a lot of time left.' And except for an ache here a pain there I feel like the proverbial spring colt. There is so much left to do . . . Your kids keep me young even if I don't bend as easily or run as fast or hear as well. . . . Maybe I am a little grumpier when there are a whole bunch of them together making funny sounds and having too many friends over who leave too many smelly sneakers around. And, yes, I confess I am less tolerant about the 7UP can barely sipped — left to get stale and warm or about all the lights left on or about the VCR's whose empty cases are strewn around, the tapes themselves off in another house — stuck into yet another VCR machine. Though I try not to show it, I

also get irritated when I go to watch a tape instead of the Hitchcock movie or my Kostner film in the proper cover I find a tape of Bambi or of that horrible Simpson family — always a tape that needs rewinding too . . . Am I being unreasonable here? I have given up trying to assign blame. I did that when you all were young but I never had my heart and soul in the blame game. Now I find I tune out when someone says, "Ask Jeb, he knows!" Or "Gampy, I wasn't in the boat when it hit the rock." Or after all five gallons of French vanilla turned to mush, the freezer door having been left open all night, "I didn't do it, and I'm not saying who did, but Robert took out two Eskimo Pies after dinner — honest!" I wasn't trying to find the culprit. I was trying to safeguard our future. I realize "Keep the freezer door closed from now on and I mean it" lacks the rhetorical depth of "This will not stand" or "Read my lips" but back in the White House days Ramsey or George worried about closing the freezer door while I worried about other problems. The lines were more clearly drawn back then. No there is a difference now, and maybe when we reconvene next year, you'll notice even more of a gentle slide. I hope not. I want to put this 'aging' on hold for a while now. I don't expect to be on the A team anymore; but I want to play golf with you. And I want to fish or throw shoes. And I want to rejoice in your victories be they political, or business, or family happiness victories . . . As the summer finishes out and the seas get a little higher, the winds is a little colder, I'll be making some notes — writing it down lest I forget — so I can add to this report on getting older. Who knows maybe they'll come out with a new drug that makes legs bend easier — joints hurt less, drives go farther, memory come roaring back, and all fears about falling off fishing rocks go away. Remember the old song "I'll be there ready when you are." Well I'll be there ready when you are, for there's so much excitement ahead, so many grandkids to watch grow. If you need me I'm here.

Devotedly,
Dad

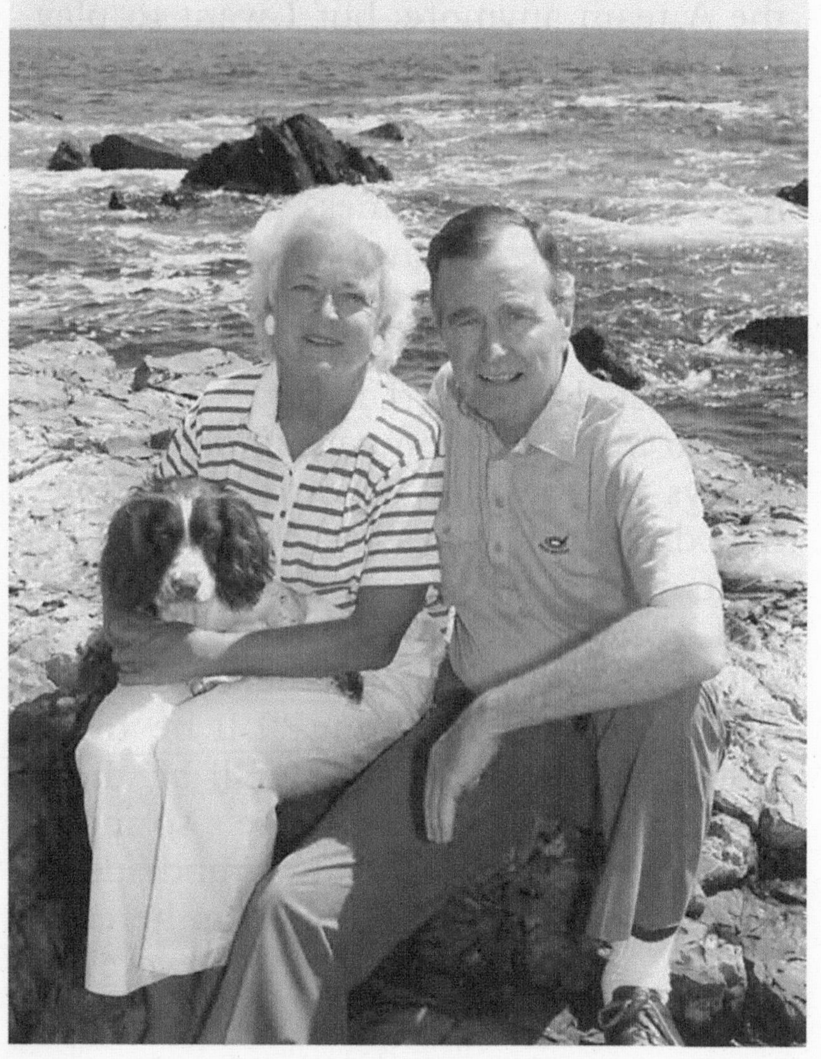

On the rocks at Walker's Point.

Twenty-One: Anchor to Windward

October 6, 2001

Dear Kids,
This is my last day in Kennebunkport after almost five months of great happiness. There is something about this place that gets into one's very soul. Don't you agree?

When you all weren't here, your mother and I would sit out on the deck at noon, just the two of us. Spoiled by Ariel we'd have a little soup or sandwich. I'd usually take a glass of very dry Spanish sherry. (I am spoiling myself more these days with good sherry and, yes, before dinner a good vodka. No more [Manishewitz] or Popov for your Dad — well unless we have guests over. You know the formula — pour the Popov into the Grey Goose bottle or the New York State sherry into the Juarez El Fino bottle. It's hard to tell.)

Anyway — where was I? I do forget a lot more. Like I wrote you four years ago I can remember long ago, but not yesterday. The other day I had an audience with the Pope. After I finished, the people I was traveling with were invited in for a photo with the Holy Father. I started introducing them as in they came one by one to receive the Pope's blessing. But along came my friend Bill Conway and I drew a blank. Then I correctly clicked off a couple, then I drew a blank on three of our USSS agents.

But forget that forgetfulness. Here's what I want to tell you at summer's end.

I had a little plaque made. It says CAVU. CAVU was the kind of weather we Navy pilots wanted when we were to fly off our carrier in the Pacific. We had little navigational instrumentation so we wanted CAVU — "Ceiling and Visibility Unlimited."

At Gar Hole's funeral this summer — he was our exec in the Pacific — I saw a wooden plaque that read CAVU, so I had a little bronze one made up for the end of our house here, the end where the seas pound into the rocks the most, the spray most likely to weather my plaque. It will then blend nicely in and guests will no longer say "What does CAVU mean?"

When it has blended in, outsiders might not notice it, fine by me. But I will not pass it by without realizing how lucky I am, for this plaque describes my own life — as it has been over the years, as it is right now.

I used to seek broad horizons in life and I found plenty. Now I don't care if I can't even see Ogunquit. Limited horizons are OK by me just so family's in view.

I don't want to sit at the head table or be honored or get a medal or have stuff named for me. That's happened and I have been truly grateful for some of the honors, but no more need come my way.

I sit on our deck, out of the wind, near the sea. And I realize that because of all five of you and yours I am a very happy man. I don't need anything. I don't want anything — only your love.

Because of your love and your caring about us and the joy of your kids' laughter and even the sadness a tear reveals, I know that my life has been very full and very happy. And your mother feels exactly the same way.

Your mother and I sit out there like a couple of really old poops, but we are at total peace. She does crossword puzzles, real puzzles, reads a ton of books, plays golf, calls people up on the phone, writes letters, is writing a book, and occasionally gets mildly (to use an old Navy expression) pissed off at me. I can handle it though — no problem. I fall back on bad hearing or changing the subject. Both work.

Because of you five whose hugs I can still feel, whose own lives have made me so proud, I can confidently tell my guardian angels that my life is CAVU; and it will be that way until the day I die — all because of you.

I love you very much.

Now I must close my suitcase and head for Sanford and get on a plane that will have us home, back in Texas tonight. But it is going to be hard to drive out our gate, because the seas are churned up by gale winds, and the bay is covered with foam driven up from the crashing waves hitting our rocks.

I can't see the notch in the hills across the ocean, the notch that I navigate by to get to Perkins Cove so in that sense visibility is less than perfect; and yet,

George's boat, Fidelity, *off Walker's Point.*

when I drive out the gate and look back at the Big House or the Bungalow I can confidently tell my kids my life is CAVU — ceiling and visibility are truly unlimited for your 77 year old, devoted, Dad.

"Kennebunkport has been my anchor to windward throughout a full and challenging life. It has kept me grounded and focused on what is really important."

— GEORGE BUSH, TO THE BOSTON GLOBE, JULY 2017

Every summer of his life except one, George H. W. Bush has visited his family's compound, Walker's Point, in Kennebunkport, Maine.

In the early twentieth century, the Bushes would take a train from Greenwich to Boston and then drive north up Route One. When the family crossed over the Piscataqua River, they'd already arrived, even with an hour drive still ahead. "In the summer we'd go for three weeks or two weeks, and I remember driving across the bridge between New Hampshire and Maine and my mother would say, 'Roll down the windows and breathe in that salt air!' and we'd roll down the windows and we felt we were breathing in the salt air, but that was kind of stability for us and I remember I loved it," said George.

He and his siblings would swim, ride bikes to the tennis courts, and get into trouble. As an adult, even when they were living in Texas, he traveled back up north. There was less mischief, but still tennis and boat rides and peace. Of course, there have been many changes, and the peninsula is not the same as it was: in 1989 it was outfitted for a president with office buildings, secret service agents, and a landing spot for *Marine One.* A house was airlifted to the peninsula for the White House physician; George purchased the house after the presidency and now Neil and his family spend time there. However, as he watches from the living room, the pulsing blue water is still restless, beautiful, and signifies coming home. Grandkids now run around the property. They organize activities like tennis and golf tournaments and boot camp workouts and stay for dinner. The next generation has

Walker's Point seen from the Shore Road in Kennebunkport, Maine. (© Heidi Kirn)

already pledged to uphold the significance of this place.

Leave downtown Kennebunkport and head north along Ocean Avenue as the Bushes have done for close to a century. With Dock Square in the rearview mirror, the Kennebunk River twists on the right. On the left, Ganny's Garden grows on the Village Green. The blooming patch of flowers was a gift from her friends and family in 2011, and it is maintained by the Kennebunkport Conservation Trust. Throughout the garden, her grandchildren's initials are hidden, just like she did on her needlepoint rug, which lies on the floor of the living room in Houston. Bronze sculptures create a frozen scene with two kicked-off mismatched Keds, a straw hat, and her favorite book *Pride and Prejudice* opened and face down — it's as if she was just there.

"I'm a nester, and that house has come to mean roots . . . When I'm in my garden in Maine, putting peonies that will last 100 years in the ground, I'm planting for generations. I'm doing that for my children and grandchildren."

— BARBARA BUSH

The Bush family in 2015. Family is always the most important thing.

A mile further up Ocean Avenue, the river pours into the ocean, the road bends at Cape Arundel, and Walker's Point comes into view. First, the Big House, shingled and worn by weather, looks as if it's on its own, facing the fury of the sea alone. Gathered near the three-story home is a collection of houses, each uniform but distinct.

Here, Ocean Avenue widens on the water side to make room for cars that have pulled over for a peek at the complex. In 2009, friends and family dedicated a 6,000-pound anchor built from a destroyer in honor of George's time-honored address. At a small ceremony, George drew laughter with his quick wit: "All this tribute and I'm not even dead yet." With his cane and an arm on his granddaughter Lauren's shoulder he walked over to read the plaque:

> "For our Friend and 41st President George H. W. Bush: 'An Anchor to Windward.' As he was for our nation and world during four years of tumultuous and historic change, so, too, has Kennebunkport served, in the words of St. Paul, 'as an anchor of the soul, both sure and steadfast' to him."

The one summer that George could not visit Walker's Point was in 1944 when he was stationed in the South Pacific. The year before was when he brought Barbara up for the first time. She was eighteen and she fell in love with George and Maine. That summer, they made a lifelong promise to one another with a secret engagement by the rocks surrounding the home. Neither George nor Barbara remember whether there was a formal ask — there was never a knelt question. Like a knowing glance across the dinner table, they just knew they wanted to be together.

In a life of ups and downs, struggles and

successes, fame and defeat, Walker's Point has served as the Bushes' constant. No matter what crisis loomed, the couple could return to Maine to watch the moon rise up from below the horizon, hear the waves crash against the coast, and breathe the fresh air together. George calls it their anchor to windward — the place they can come home to, and while the town may change, kids grow older, and life progresses, the house on the point remains and calls them back home.

Love is defined by the people who hold it. At first, it is all-consuming and full of hope and courage, and blazes wildly like a bonfire. But if young love is a bonfire then old love is the beacon. Rooted into the landscape, not roaring all at once, but casting a slow and steady beam that guides ships back home to a safe harbor.

As the page turns to October and the chill in the air lingers longer, the Bushes begin boarding up Walker's Point. The beds are stripped, sheets and blankets are stowed away, and mementos are placed into boxes. Furniture is covered in plastic, mothballs go into closets, the pool is drained, and *Fidelity* is hauled out of the water. The compound empties for the winter ahead and they fly south to Texas.

Before they go — one last sit on the porch in a sunny spot, another walk along the beach bundled up, and a final sip of the salt air. They've done it many times before, but it's always hard to say good-bye to this grounding, gathering place.

They move slower through the rooms of this old house. Time has caused their bodies to ache more. Barbara is on a breathing machine and George is confined to a wheelchair. Three-quarters of a century together, they grasp only what is most important.

The authors (Ellie left, Kelly right) with George and Barbara at Walker's Point, 2017.

"I've been holding his hand a lot more these days," said Barbara.

Seventy-six years later, they still reach for each other's hands. They've both been in and out of the hospital, but no matter who is hurting, the other sits beside them — their hands clasped. His hand is "fat and squishy" laughs Barbara, and she knows just where to find it.

Recently, their doctor suggested that they consider sleeping in separate beds because rest is so important at their age. But they refused for as long as possible. George argued that when he woke in the middle of the night, he needed to be able to reach out and know that Barbara was there.

SOURCES

Chapter 1

1. "We always had to go into Mother's room . . ." Barbara Bush, *Barbara Bush: A Memoir,* A Lisa Drew Book/Scribner, 1994, p. 17.
2. "the life of the party." Jeffrey Roth, *41,* Documentary. June 2012; New York and London: Playground Productions/HBO.
3. Who's that? asked a young George "Poppy" Bush. That's Barbara Pierce from Rye, said Jack Wozencraft, a mutual friend who then offered an introduction. George Bush with Victor Gold, *Looking Forward,* Doubleday, 1987, p. 31.
4. Can't this wait until morning? Barbara's father, Marvin Pierce, called from the next bed. Barbara Bush, *Barbara Bush: A Memoir,* A Lisa Drew Book/Scribner, 1994, p. 16–17.
5. "very nice family," Ibid.

Chapter 2

1. "I've banned the 'L' word . . ." David Baldacci, "George and Barbara Bush" *Parade Magazine,* December 13, 2009.
2. "a basic green line wrapped around a wooden rack . . ." George Bush with Victor Gold, *Looking Forward,* Doubleday, 1987, p. 29.
3. "Bringing one in, especially a green beauty . . ." Ibid.
4. "I loved the physical sensation of steering a powerful machine . . ." Ibid.
5. "Life gets so hectic that I feel . . ." "Dear Mrs. Lindbergh," *Connecticut Life,* May 4, 1961.
6. "studies, play, and character." Douglas Lyons, "Manners, Marbles, Morals," GCDS Headmaster 1992–2004, on the history of The Greenwich Country Day School, www.gcds.net/about/mission-history-future.
7. "dominated free time and after-school time." Ibid.
8. "generated great excitement as marbles were won . . ." Ibid.
9. . . . by the family driver. Jon Meacham, *Destiny and Power: The American Odyssey of George Herbert Walker Bush,* Random House 2015, p. 28.

10. "big, strong, principled" Doro Bush Koch, *My Father, My President: A Personal Account of the Life of George H. W. Bush,* Warner Books, 2006 p. 5.
11. "wasn't cozy like Mother," Ibid., p. 6.
12. "Dad taught us about duty and service. Mother taught us . . ." George Bush with Victor Gold, *Looking Forward,* Doubleday, 1987, p. 26.
13. "Thinking she was joking, the friend quit . . ." George W. Bush, *41: A Portrait of My Father,* Crown Publishers, 2014, p. 7.
14. "I pointed out that as a candidate . . ." George Bush with Victor Gold, *Looking Forward,* Doubleday, 1987, pp. 26–27.
15. "[My mother] had these kind of truisms that served me . . ." Jeffrey Roth, *41,* Documentary. June 2012; New York and London: Playground Productions/HBO.

Chapter 3

1. Her whole family had a suspicious interest. . . . Barbara Bush, *Barbara Bush: A Memoir,* A Lisa Drew Book/Scribner, 1994, p. 17.
2. "sit in stony silence . . ." Ibid.
3. "obviously had been to . . ." Ibid.

Chapter 4

1. "The stranger who climbs to Andover Hill . . ." Claude Moore Fuess, *An Old New England School: A History of Phillips Academy Andover,* Houghton Mifflin Company, 1917, p. 448.
2. "It has been the ambition of the school . . ." Ibid, p. 486.
3. His marks were low and his performance in the classroom . . . Jon Meacham, *Destiny and Power: The American Odyssey of George Herbert Walker Bush,* Random House 2015, pp. 34–35.
4. It didn't help when in April of 1940 . . . Ibid, pp. 34–35.
5. At the suggestion of a teacher . . . Ibid, p. 35.
6. "That year was the making of George . . ." Doro Bush Koch, *My Father, My President: A Personal Account of the Life of George H.W. Bush,* Warner Books, 2006, p. 12.
7. . . . partially influenced by a trip to New York for Fleet Week . . . Jon Meacham, *Destiny and Power: The American Odyssey of George Herbert Walker Bush,* Random House 2015, p. 39.

Chapter 5

1. "Some of my happiest memories . . ." Barbara Bush, *Barbara Bush: A Memoir,* A Lisa Drew Book/Scribner, 1994, p. 5.
2. "[My father] was the fairest man . . ." Ibid, p. 7.
3. "smiling man" Ibid.
4. "That way I avoided being the last girl . . ." Ibid, p. 13.
5. "when her ship came in," Ibid, p. 9.
6. "You have two choices in life . . ." Ibid.
7. "Eat up, Martha. Not you, Barbara!" Ibid, pp. 6–7.
8. "produce an educated woman who is independent . . ." Ileana Strauch, *Ashley Hall,* Arcadia Publishing, 2003, p. 120.
9. "Gloves and hats had to be worn . . ." Ibid, p. 108.
10. "Pearls and Amethyst," Ibid, p. 121.
11. "In an Oak-Shaded Garden." Ibid, p. 104.
12. "uninvited" and "forced to bake cookies for the seniors . . ." Ibid, p. 55.
13. "unpatriotic" Barbara Bush, *Barbara Bush: A Memoir,* A Lisa Drew Book/ Scribner, 1994, p. 18.

Chapter 6

1. "Like most people in the country, I wanted to participate . . ." Jeffrey Roth, *41,* Documentary. June 2012; New York and London: Playground Productions/HBO.
2. "[He] advised my class to go . . ." George Bush, *All the Best, George Bush: My Life in Letters and Other Writings,* Scribner, 2013, p. 23.
3. "George — did the Secretary say anything to change your mind?" "No, sir. I'm going in." George Bush with Victor Gold, *Looking Forward,* Doubleday, 1987, p. 30.
4. "My father took me down to Pennsylvania Station in New York . . ." Jeffrey Roth, *41,* Documentary. June 2012; New York and London: Playground Productions/HBO.
5. "Now about your question, Mum . . ." George Bush. George Bush to Dorothy Walker Bush, Chapel Hill, North Carolina, undated. President Bush's letter was not dated at this time, but he was in training in Chapel Hill in the fall of 1942.
6. "For a kiss to mean engagement is a very beautiful idea, Mama . . ." George Bush. George Bush to Dorothy Walker Bush, Chapel Hill, North Carolina, undated.
7. "He wrote and asked me to please tell

everyone . . ." Barbara Bush, *Barbara Bush: A Memoir,* A Lisa Drew Book/ Scribner, 1994, p. 18.

8. "Well today sure was wonderful . . . I met Barbara at the Inn at 12 . . ." George Bush. George Bush to Dorothy Walker Bush, Chapel Hill, North Carolina, undated.
9. "She sent him one that was several years old and featured my cairn puppy . . ." Barbara Bush, *Barbara Bush: A Memoir,* A Lisa Drew Book/Scribner, 1994, p. 18.
10. "Thanksgiving comes tomorrow. I guess that I will hardly notice it here . . ." George Bush. George Bush to Dorothy Walker Bush, Minneapolis, Minnesota, November 25, 1942.
11. "It's days like this that makes me anxious to be out fighting — though I know I can never become a killer . . ." George Bush. George Bush to Dorothy Walker Bush, Minneapolis, Minnesota, undated.
12. "I got a letter from F. Von Stade . . ." George Bush. George Bush to Dorothy Walker Bush, Corpus Christi, Texas, undated. George Bush was in Corpus Christi, Texas, from February to June 1943.
13. "Mum, I'm really worried. I hope it's

one of her lapses . . ." George Bush. George Bush to Dorothy Walker Bush, Corpus Christi, Texas, undated.

Chapter 7

1. "I guess Mrs. Bush had all sorts of reasons . . ." Barbara Bush, *Barbara Bush: A Memoir,* A Lisa Drew Book/Scribner, 1994, p. 19.
2. "That was my first trip to Kennebunkport, Maine . . ." Ibid.
3. "George's brother Pres used to tease me . . ." Ibid.
4. "George invariably wanted to go sailing . . ." Joe Hyams, *Flight of the Avenger,* G. K. Hall & Co., 1991, p. 72.
5. "One last thing, sweet Mama! . . ." George Bush. George Bush to Dorothy Walker Bush, undated.

Chapter 8

1. "Mr. Bush and I wanted to send you this token . . ." Dorothy Walker Bush. Dorothy Walker Bush to Barbara Pierce, Greenwich, Connecticut, undated.
2. "Mother telephoned you this morning . . ." Marvin Pierce. Marvin Pierce to Barbara Pierce, New York City, New York,

undated.

3. "My darling Bar . . ." George Bush. George Bush to Barbara Pierce, December 12, 1943.

Chapter 9

1. "This is the last farewell I guess, Mum . . ." George Bush. George Bush to Dorothy Walker Bush, March 28, 1944.
2. On April 20, 1944, the *San Jac* reached Pearl Harbor . . . Jon Meacham, *Destiny and Power: The American Odyssey of George Herbert Walker Bush,* Random House 2015, p. 57.
3. "The ships were still in the water . . ." President George H. W. Bush, "Speech at Pearl Harbor," 1999, George Bush Presidential Library and Museum.
4. By May, the *San Jac* had reached its destination . . . Jon Meacham, *Destiny and Power: The American Odyssey of George Herbert Walker Bush,* Random House, 2015, p. 57.
5. "Here is some distressing news . . ." George Bush. George Bush to Dorothy Bush, May 26, 1944.
6. "What are your plans . . ." George Bush. George Bush to Dorothy Bush, June 10, 1944.

Chapter 10

1. "Being out at sea is always exciting and fortunately . . ." George Bush. George Bush to Dorothy Walker Bush, May 26, 1944.
2. Understanding the importance of . . . "V-Mail," Smithsonian National Postal Museum, postalmuseum.si.edu/exhibits/past/the-art-of-cards-and-letters/mail-call/v-mail.html.
3. Those letters were sent to . . . Ibid.
4. The reels of film were then delivered . . . Ibid.
5. At the stations, letters were . . . Ibid.
6. "We were frantic" Barbara Bush, *Barbara Bush: A Memoir,* A Lisa Drew Book/ Scribner, 1994, p. 23.
7. A large explosion came from . . . Joe Hyams, *Flight of the Avenger,* G. K. Hall & Co., 1991, p. 144.
8. George abandoned the *Avenger* 2,000 feet about the water . . . Joe Hyams, *Flight of the Avenger,* G. K. Hall & Co., 1991, p. 160–61.
9. "I had some dye marker attached to my life jacket . . ." George Bush. George Bush to Dorothy Walker Bush and Prescott Bush, September 3, 1944.
10. "what appeared to be . . ." George Bush

with Victor Gold, *Looking Forward,* Doubleday, 1987, p. 38.

11. "The dot grew larger . . ." Ibid.
12. "Let's get below . . ." Ibid.
13. "utterly useless" and "sweep the sea and skies pretty well" George Bush. George Bush to Dorothy Walker Bush and Prescott Bush, September 5, 1944.
14. "The sub moved like a porpoise . . ." George Bush with Victor Gold, *Looking Forward,* Doubleday, 1987, p. 40.
15. It reminded me . . . Ibid.
16. "I still don't understand the "logic" of war . . ." Ibid.

Chapter 11

1. "All during the time I was talking . . ." George Bush. George Bush to Dorothy Walker Bush, November 3, 1944.
2. "rarely went into the city" Barbara Bush, *Barbara Bush: A Memoir,* A Lisa Drew Book/Scribner, 1994, p. 22.
3. "He talked to me about marriage . . ." Ibid.
4. "He also told me that the three most important things . . ." Ibid, p. 23.
5. "No reunion could have been . . ." George Bush with Victor Gold, *Looking Forward,* Doubleday, 1987, p. 40.

6. "I am so very lucky having . . ." George Bush. George Bush to Dorothy Bush, undated.

Chapter 12

1. Yale readmitted all 1,500 men who had deferred as well as 900 who left for the war as freshman . . . Judith Schiff, "Yale After the War," *Yale Alumni Magazine,* July/August 2016.
2. "I do not remember many of the details . . ." Barbara Bush, *Barbara Bush: A Memoir,* A Lisa Drew Book/Scribner, 1994, p. 26.
3. "There are a lot of jokes about . . ." Ibid, p. 27.
4. "He could barely talk . . ." Wayne Coffey, "Recalling Poppy Bush," *New York Daily News,* June 19, 1988.
5. "a little high and outside" Maureen Dowd, "Bush Takes Mubarak Out to the Ball Game," *New York Times,* April 4, 1989.
6. "Breaking away meant just that . . ." George Bush with Victor Gold, *Looking Forward,* Doubleday, 1987, p. 23.
7. "No matter how we looked at it . . ." Ibid.
8. "Dear Gerry, We have a while . . ." George Bush. George Bush to Gerry Be-

miss, June 1948. George Bush, *All the Best, George Bush: My Life in Letters and Other Writings,* Scribner, 2013, p. 61–63.

Chapter 13

1. "This West Texas is a fabulous . . ." George Bush. George Bush to Gerry Bemiss, January 1949.
2. In 1901, the first geyser . . . Lawrence Wright, "The Dark Bounty of Texas Oil," *New Yorker,* January 2018.
3. seventeen million barrels that first year . . . Ibid.
4. "the place for ambitious young people." George Bush with Victor Gold, *Looking Forward,* Doubleday, 1987, p. 46.
5. "There's not much salary . . ." Ibid, p. 47.
6. "As far as my mother was concerned . . ." Barbara Bush, *Barbara Bush: A Memoir,* A Lisa Drew Book/Scribner, 1994, p. 32.
7. "I don't like to brag . . ." Barbara Bush. Barbara Bush to Marvin and Pauline Pierce, September 6, 1948.
8. "Bar is still not quite up to par . . ." George Bush. George Bush to Dorothy Bush, October 20, 1948.
9. "I'd load up my car with bits . . ." George Bush with Victor Gold, *Looking Forward,*

Doubleday, 1987, p. 56

10. "Sudden death is a terrible shock . . ." Barbara Bush, *Barbara Bush: A Memoir,* A Lisa Drew Book/Scribner, 1994, p. 36.
11. "Midland is a fine town . . ." George Bush. George Bush to Gerry Bemiss, January 1, 1951. George Bush, *All the Best, George Bush: My Life in Letters and Other Writings,* Scribner, 2013, p. 70.
12. "There wasn't anything subtle . . ." George Bush with Victor Gold, *Looking Forward,* Doubleday, 1987, p. 58.
13. "We were all in the same situation . . ." Susan Watters, "Feisty lady." *WWD,* October 1988.
14. "Bush is a director . . ." "Texas JayCees Name Midlander For Honor," *The Midland Reporter-Telegram,* December 30, 1956.

Chapter 14

1. Well, let's do something. What do we do? Amy Cunningham, "Good-Bye to Robin," *Texas Monthly,* February 1988.
2. "[Dr. Wyvell] gave us the best advice anyone . . ." Ibid.
3. "I remember asking the doctor why. . . ." Ibid.
4. "George didn't let me retreat." Susan

Watters, "Feisty lady." *WWD,* October 1988.

5. "Dear Mum, I have jotted . . ." George Bush. George Bush to Dorothy Walker Bush, undated. George Bush, *All the Best, George Bush: My Life in Letters and Other Writings,* Scribner, 2013, pp. 81–82.
6. "We loved our life in Midland . . ." George Bush, *All the Best, George Bush: My Life in Letters and Other Writings,* Scribner, 2013, p. 82.
7. "I spent half of the next ten years . . ." Barbara Bush, *Barbara Bush: A Memoir,* A Lisa Drew Book/Scribner, 1994, p. 55.
8. "We have Ray and Harry Hoagland . . ." Barbara Bush. Barbara Bush to family, October 1963.

Chapter 15

1. "Wherever I was, whatever I did . . ." George Bush. George Bush to C. Fred Chambers, November 14, 1972. George Bush, *All the Best, George Bush: My Life in Letters and Other Writings,* Scribner, 2013, p. 162.
2. "The argument made pragmatic sense . . ." George Bush with Victor Gold, *Looking Forward,* Doubleday, 1987, pp. 83–84.

3. "I know from this meeting . . ." Barbara Bush. Barbara Bush to family, September 1963.
4. "Bush's unique appeal . . ." Jay Milner, "A Yank Runs in Texas," *New York Herald Tribune,* September 12, 1964.
5. "The days are getting closer . . ." Barbara Bush. Barbara Bush to Taylor Blanton, January 6, 1966.
6. "Dearest George, Not much news . . ." Barbara Bush. Barbara Bush to George W. Bush, January 25, 1966.
7. "I resigned as chairman and CEO of Zapata . . ." Ibid, p. 89.

Chapter 16

1. "I love people, and . . ." Merikaye Presley, "He Can't Beat Around Bush," *Dallas Morning News,* March 28, 1970.
2. "One day I came downstairs to find George . . ." Barbara Bush, *Barbara Bush: A Memoir,* A Lisa Drew Book/Scribner, 1994, p. 64.
3. He was appointed to serve . . . Jon Meacham, *Destiny and Power: The American Odyssey of George Herbert Walker Bush,* Random House 2015, p. 133.
4. "This was a very interesting time . . ."

Barbara Bush, *Barbara Bush: A Memoir,* A Lisa Drew Book/Scribner, 1994, p. 71.

5. "What this Bill does do in this area . . ." George Bush. "Speech at Memorial High School," April 17, 1968, Memorial High School, Houston, Texas.
6. "Booed before the talk . . ." Ken Shrets, "Bush Says Life Threatened by Civil Rights Bill," *Houston Chronicle,* April 18, 1968.
7. "You have to learn in Washington . . ." Barbara Bush, *Barbara Bush: A Memoir,* A Lisa Drew Book/Scribner, 1994, p. 67.
8. "It was a strange life . . ." Ibid, p. 68.
9. "Because Dad's schedule was . . ." Doro Bush Koch, *My Father, My President: A Personal Account of the Life of George H. W. Bush,* Warner Books, 2006, p. 55.
10. "I know my claim to fame . . ." Kathy Lewis, "Don't Tell George I Told You . . ." *The Houston Post,* May 9, 1976.
11. "is the hang in there as a wife and mother." Merikaye Presley, "He Can't Beat Around Bush," *Dallas Morning News,* March 28, 1970.
12. "My feelings are kind of mixed . . ." George Bush Tape Recorded Diary, December 11, 1970. George Bush, *All the Best, George Bush: My Life in Letters and Other Writings,* Scribner, 2013, p. 133.

13. "At the time, it was home to Mrs. Douglas MacArthur . . ." Barbara Bush, *Barbara Bush: A Memoir,* A Lisa Drew Book/Scribner, 1994, p. 84.
14. "Would somebody tell me . . ." Ibid.
15. "I thought the U.N. would have some real appeal . . ." George Bush Tape Recorded Diary, December 11, 1970. George Bush, *All the Best, George Bush: My Life in Letters and Other Writings,* Scribner, 2013, p. 132.
16. "Our life in N.Y.C. is extraordinary . . ." Barbara Bush. Barbara Bush to Taylor Blanton, July 3, 1971.
17. "heart and soul wrapped up . . ." George Bush. George Bush to Sally McKenzie, November 5, 1971. George Bush, *All the Best, George Bush: My Life in Letters and Other Writings,* Scribner, 2013, p. 154.
18. "it was a dark moment . . ." George Bush, *All the Best, George Bush: My Life in Letters and Other Writings,* Scribner, 2013, p. 153.
19. "Poor Mom. The rice was . . ." Barbara Bush, *Barbara Bush: A Memoir,* A Lisa Drew Book/Scribner, 1994, p. 92
20. "Dear Mr. President, . . ." George Bush. George Bush to Richard Nixon, November 21, 1972. George Bush, *All the Best,*

George Bush: My Life in Letters and Other Writings, Scribner, 2013, pp. 162–63.

21. George traveled close to 100,000 miles and visited 33 states in one year. Jon Meacham, *Destiny and Power: The American Odyssey of George Herbert Walker Bush,* Random House 2015, p. 164.
22. "Mail poured into the RNC office . . ." George Bush, *All the Best, George Bush: My Life in Letters and Other Writings,* Scribner, 2013, p. 165.
23. "Dear Mr. President, It is my considered judgment . . ." Ibid, p. 193.
24. "There is no way to really describe the emotion . . ." George Bush Diary, August 9, 1974; George Bush, *All the Best, George Bush: My Life in Letters and Other Writings,* Scribner, 2013, pp. 194–195.

Chapter 17

1. "I miss you more than tongue can tell . . ." George Bush. George Bush to Barbara Bush, December 22, 1974.
2. "The more George talked, the more excited . . ." Barbara Bush, *Barbara Bush: A Memoir,* A Lisa Drew Book/Scribner, 1994, p. 109.
3. "We're here. We have been for almost four

fascinating weeks . . ." George Bush. George Bush to James Baker, November 17, 1974. George Bush, *All the Best, George Bush: My Life in Letters and Other Writings,* Scribner, 2013, p. 207.

4. "felt it was best to have a small mission, keep a low profile" George Bush Diary, October 21, 1974. George Bush, *All the Best, George Bush: My Life in Letters and Other Writings,* Scribner, 2013, p. 200.
5. "My hyper-adrenaline, political instincts . . ." Ibid.
6. "The Algerian ambassador looked . . ." Ibid, p. 204.
7. Barbara had decided . . . Barbara Bush, *Barbara Bush: A Memoir,* A Lisa Drew Book/Scribner, 1994, p. 126.
8. "We rode into the southern part . . ." Barbara Bush. Barbara Bush to family, November 1974.
9. "Great talks with Bar on the phone . . ." George Bush Diary, December 4, 1974. George Bush, *All the Best, George Bush: My Life in Letters and Other Writings,* Scribner, 2013, p. 211.
10. "Dear Bar . . . I love you. It's bad being . . ." George Bush. George Bush to Barbara Bush, December 16, 1974.
11. "17 days have gone by since . . ." Barbara Bush. Barbara Bush to family, No-

vember 19, 1975.

12. "He cannot share this part . . ." Barbara Bush. Barbara Bush to family, January 30, 1976.
13. "I was very depressed, lonely, and unhappy." Barbara Bush, *Barbara Bush: A Memoir,* A Lisa Drew Book/Scribner, 1994, p. 137.
14. "Night after night George . . ." Ibid.
15. "My 'code' told me . . ." Ibid.

Chapter 18

1. "George Bush has been actively running . . ." Barbara Bush diary, September 18, 1978.
2. "George and I are traveling . . ." Barbara Bush. Barbara Bush to Taylor Blanton, March 1, 1979.
3. "One very good thing came out . . ." Barbara Bush, *Barbara Bush: A Memoir,* A Lisa Drew Book/Scribner, 1994, p. 149.
4. "I saw Barbara twice this week . . ." George Bush Diary, September 29, 1979. George Bush, *All the Best, George Bush: My Life in Letters and Other Writings,* Scribner, 2013, p. 282.
5. "Happy happy 54th . . ." George Bush. George Bush to Barbara Bush, June 8, 1979.

6. "We came to this convention to leave politics . . ." Barbara Bush, *Barbara Bush: A Memoir,* A Lisa Drew Book/Scribner, 1994, p. 156.
7. "There was never a hint of negative feeling . . ." George Bush with Victor Gold, *Looking Forward,* Doubleday, 1987, p. 222.
8. "You're not going to be sorry . . ." Jon Meacham, *Destiny and Power: The American Odyssey of George Herbert Walker Bush,* Random House 2015, p. 254.
9. "We're using it as a home . . ." "A Tour of the Vice Presidential Residence with Mrs. George Bush," *Capitol Hill: Magazine of the National Republican Club,* Winter 1983.
10. "George and I traveled an estimated 1.3 million miles . . ." Barbara Bush, *Barbara Bush: A Memoir,* A Lisa Drew Book/Scribner, 1994, p. 169.
11. "Only the president lands . . ." George Bush with Victor Gold, *Looking Forward,* Doubleday, 1987, p. 225.
12. "I really needed to hear his voice . . ." Barbara Bush, *Barbara Bush: A Memoir,* A Lisa Drew Book/Scribner, 1994, p. 167.
13. "He gave me a hug . . ." Ibid, p. 168.
14. "George said that was easy as . . ." Ibid, p. 207.

15. "It was a 41st wedding . . ." Ibid.
16. "Let's see Bar — 42 years ago . . ." George Bush. George Bush to Barbara Bush, January 6th, 1987. George Bush, *All the Best, George Bush: My Life in Letters and Other Writings,* Scribner, 2013, p. 357.
17. "Of course it wasn't true . . ." Doro Bush Koch, *My Father, My President: A Personal Account of the Life of George H. W. Bush,* Warner Books, 2006, p. 224.
18. "Bush's handlers argued . . ." Margaret Carlson, "The Silver Fox," *TIME,* January 21, 1989.
19. "I still find it incredible . . ." Doro Bush Koch, *My Father, My President: A Personal Account of the Life of George H. W. Bush,* Warner Books, 2006 p. 253.
20. "I awakened this morning . . ." Barbara Bush, *Barbara Bush: A Memoir,* A Lisa Drew Book/Scribner, 1994, p. 250.

Chapter 19

1. "After eight years of new-money flash and glitz . . ." Margaret Carlson, "The Silver Fox," *TIME,* January 21, 1989.
2. "We get enormous strength . . ." Bernard Weintraub, "A Down-to-Earth-Tenant for an Exclusive Address, *New York Times,* January 15, 1989.

3. "Kuwait is liberated . . ." War Summary, *New York Times,* February 28, 1991.
4. "Dear George, Jeb, Neil, Marvin, Doro . . ." George Bush. George Bush to George W. Bush, Jeb Bush, Neil Bush, Marin Bush, and Doro LeBlond, December 31, 1990.
5. "According to them: 'Barbara Bush . . ." Barbara Bush, *Barbara Bush: A Memoir,* A Lisa Drew Book/Scribner, 1994, p. 341.
6. "This is all extraordinarily tough . . ." George Bush, *All the Best, George Bush: My Life in Letters and Other Writings,* Scribner, 2013, p. 568.

Chapter 20

1. "Then came the moment when the mantle . . ." Barbara Bush, *Barbara Bush: A Memoir,* A Lisa Drew Book/Scribner, 1994, p. 3
2. "Barbara is wonderful . . ." George Bush, *All the Best, George Bush: My Life in Letters and Other Writings,* Scribner, 2013, pp. 583–84.
3. "Will you marry me? . . ." George Bush. George Bush to Barbara Bush. January 6, 1994.
4. "Last year there was only . . ." George Bush. George Bush to George W. Bush,

John Ellis Bush, Marvin Bush, Neil Bush, and Dorothy Bush Koch. September 23, 1998.

Chapter 21

1. "This is my last day in Kennebunkport . . ." George Bush. George Bush to George W. Bush, John Ellis Bush, Marvin Bush, Neil Bush, and Dorothy Bush Koch. October 6, 2001.
2. "Kennebunkport has been my anchor . . ." Brian MacQuarrie, "Kennebunkport loves the Bushes. The feeling is mutual," *Boston Globe,* July 3, 2017.
3. "In the summer we'd go for three . . ." Jeffrey Roth, *41,* Documentary. June 2012; New York and London: Playground Productions/HBO.
4. "When I'm in my garden in Maine . . ." Susan Watters, "Feisty lady." *WWD,* October 1988.

ABOUT THE AUTHORS

President and Mrs. Bush's granddaughter, **Ellie LeBlond Sosa**, is based in Boston, Massachusetts, where she works for a healthcare nonprofit. Her passion, though, lies in health and wellness. She earned her certificate as a holistic health counselor in 2013 and teaches fitness in Boston as well as on retreats for women around the world. Ellie met her husband of four years at her grandparents' home in Kennebunkport, Maine, and was married there in 2014. Her grandparents' love story is one that she looks up to and strives to emulate in her own life.

Kelly Anne Chase is a New England–based writer and magazine editor. She earned her bachelor's degree in history from American University and her master's in publishing and writing from Emerson College. She lives with her husband on the South Shore of Massachusetts.

The employees of Thorndike Press hope you have enjoyed this Large Print book. All our Thorndike, Wheeler, and Kennebec Large Print titles are designed for easy reading, and all our books are made to last. Other Thorndike Press Large Print books are available at your library, through selected bookstores, or directly from us.

For information about titles, please call:

(800) 223-1244

or visit our website at:

gale.com/thorndike

To share your comments, please write:

Publisher
Thorndike Press
10 Water St., Suite 310
Waterville, ME 04901